6 HALLMARKS OF A
FANTASTIC
FOURTH
QUARTER

Your Master Plan for Finishing Strong©
A *When It's Time*® Resource

RICK CRAIG

© 2025 Rick Craig

Published by Bella Matt Press, www.whenitstime.org

All rights reserved, including the right to reproduce this book or portions thereof in any form whatsoever. For permission requests, write to the author at pastorrickcraig@whenitstime.org.

No representation is made as to the legal validity or accuracy of any provision for any particular situation. If you desire medical, legal, or tax advice, consult an appropriate professional.

Due to the changing nature of the internet, any web addresses, links, or URLs listed in this book may have been altered and may no longer be accessible.

For information about special discounts for bulk purchases, please contact the author at pastorrickcraig@whenitstime.org.

Unless otherwise noted, all Scripture quotations taken from The Holy Bible, New International Version®, NIV®. Copyright © 1973, 1978, 1984, 2011 by Biblica, Inc. Used with permission of Zondervan. All rights reserved worldwide. www.zondervan.com

Scripture quotations marked (ESV) are from The Holy Bible, English Standard Version ® (ESV ®), copyright © 2001 by Crossway, a publishing ministry of Good News Publishers. Used by permission. All rights reserved.

Produced by Inksnatcher.com

Author photo: Lea Dawn Photography

LCCN record available at https://lccn.loc.gov / Library of Congress Cataloging-in-Publication Data

Names: Craig, Rick, author

Title: 6 Hallmarks of a Fantastic Fourth Quarter: Your Master Plan for Finishing Strong / Rick Craig

Subjects: | BISAC: HEALTH & FITNESS / Aging & Longevity | SELF-HELP / Aging | RELIGION / Christian Living / Personal Growth

Description: First edition. | Bella Matt Press, Fairfield, CA, 2025. | Summary: A practical and faith-filled guide that equips people to finish life's final season with wholeness and a lasting spiritual legacy. —Provided by publisher.

Identifiers: LCCN 2025923788 | 979-8-9883855-3-0 (paperback) | 979-8-9883855-4-7 (e-book)

Printed in the United States of America

To finish strong is to live with purpose, to face change with courage, and to choose legacy over comfort. It is a rare path, but those who walk it give their loved ones something far greater than memories: They give them clarity, peace, and hope.

CONTENTS

PREFACE

Why call this book *The Fourth Quarter*? The term has multiple references, such as the fourth quarter in a football or basketball game, or in this instance, the fourth and final quarter of our lives. If we break out life expectancy into quarters, the average fourth quarter for men begins at age fifty-six and ends about seventy-five, and for women, it begins at sixty years old and ends around the age of eighty. I, along with my six coauthors, will focus on this fourth quarter of life.

The fourth quarter brings unique challenges as well as opportunities. In these pages, we'll explore how to approach it with intention through six hallmark areas: emotional health, relational richness, physical fitness, vocational alignment, financial freedom, and spiritual anchoring. We will conclude with insights into remaining teachable in this fourth quarter, and with the writing of a legacy letter for those you love.

In reference to the term *hallmarks*, the term originally referred to official marks stamped on articles made of precious metals, such as gold and silver, to certify and guarantee their purity, quality, and authenticity, ensuring that the item met specific standards set by a governing body. In a broader and more metaphorical sense, the concept of hallmarks has been extended beyond the stamps on precious metals to refer to distinguishing features or characteristics that serve as indicators of quality, authenticity, or a particular identity. This is applied in various contexts:

Character Traits: Traits such as integrity, honesty, trustworthiness, and compassion are often seen as hallmarks of a person's character. These traits distinguish an individual and reflect their moral and ethical standards. Hallmarks such as these are also found extensively in the Bible, highlighted as precepts for living an honorable, humble, and distinguished life.

Professional Excellence: When it comes to reliability, innovation, and expertise, a product or service's hallmark can be measured and known for setting or meeting high standards within its industry—through achievements, meritorious results, high quality, and longevity.

Historical Events: Hallmarks define periods in history, such as the innovation and progress of the Industrial Revolution, or the productivity, ingenuity, and commitment of the greatest generation—those who grew up during the Great Depression and served in World War II. Hallmarks also mark cultural and legal changes, such as the Emancipation Proclamation in 1862—freeing millions of slaves—or women's right to vote. These historical hallmarks led to changes for the better.

Academic Standards: The hallmarks of a prestigious institution or medical institution might include rigorous academic programs, a distinguished faculty, and a strong tradition of research and scholarship. All of these attributes are easily tracked and verified, and as a result, their hallmarks can withstand the scrutiny of contentious debate.

Everyday Application: Recognizing hallmarks can help individuals make informed decisions, whether choosing a product or service provider, evaluating someone's character, or understanding the significance of a cultural artifact.

Given the variety of hallmarks, I knew writing the entire book alone would be too daunting. The best and only option was to invite the finest in their fields to coauthor it. Together, seven experts—Dr. Charity Byers and Dr. John Walker, psychologists; Dr. Bill Nesbitt, physician; Lynne Nachtrieb, dietitian; Scott Couchenour, executive coach; Kent Kuhlmann, financial advisor; and I (Rick), pastor and previous business owner—offer insight and guidance for fourth-quarter living.

Because six of the seven authors are in their fourth quarter and one is in their third quarter, they speak from experience, gleaning from their past and sharing what they have learned for your benefit. Each author has written in their personal voice and style, expressing themselves freely. Their experience is communicated through stories, examples, exercises for the reader, and encouragement to view the fourth quarter of life as an opportunity for positive change and not to accept the status quo as normal and unchangeable.

If you have read my book series titled *When It's Time®, End-of-Life Planning at Any Age: Make it Part of Your Legacy; When It's Time®, An End-of-Life Workbook for Pre-Planners and Survivors; and When It's Time®, Leader's Guide: Leading Your Group through End-of-Life Pre-Planning and Survivor Support,* then you know I am fully committed to helping people make a plan for living well now and for the end of life. Your legacy depends upon it.

—*Rick Craig*

PREPARING THE HEART FOR THE FOURTH QUARTER

A s you begin this book, I want to thank you for your willingness to pursue personal reflection and growth, and for your commitment to finishing strong in the fourth quarter of life. Whether you are just entering this season or well into its rhythms, I believe there are still opportunities to embrace deeper purpose and to shape a legacy marked by intentional living.

To begin well, we must begin from within. The fourth quarter of life doesn't ask less of us emotionally; it asks for something different. It calls us to become more intentional, more grounded, and more whole. That's why this journey starts with emotional health. I invited Dr. Charity Byers and Dr. John Walker—two respected psychologists and dear friends—to write the opening chapter, "Emotionally Healthy." Their wisdom and compassionate insight will guide you through the landscape of your inner world in this season of life—one of past wounds, present habits, emotional patterns, and the power of self-leadership.

Once we've tended to the inner life, we naturally turn to the people around us. That's where chapter 2, "Relationally Rich," picks up. Relationships matter profoundly in this season. I will walk with you through the process of reflecting on your current connections, identifying the virtues that shape meaningful relationships, and evaluating who you invite into your inner circle. It's a sacred and sometimes challenging audit, but one that can bring peace, freedom, and renewed joy.

The order of these chapters is intentional, as emotional health prepares us for relational strength. Without tending to what's unresolved within us, we risk carrying old pain into new connections. But with a heart anchored in emotional maturity, we can show up in our relationships with grace, humility, and purpose.

So, wherever you find yourself right now, take a breath. Set your heart toward growth. And know that you're not alone on this journey. We walk together—with wisdom from others, strength from God, and the courage to finish well.

—*Rick Craig*

CHAPTER 1

EMOTIONALLY HEALTHY

By Doctors Charity Byers and John Walker

It is both an honor and joy to introduce Dr. Charity Byers and Dr. John Walker—two trusted friends, wise confidants, and highly respected psychologists. Charity and John bring a powerful blend of professional expertise and deep personal insight into what it means to live with emotional balance, resilience, and purpose. Over the years, their thoughtful counsel and compassionate presence have enriched my life and the lives of many others. They approach the subject of emotional health with a combination of wisdom that speaks to both the heart and the mind, always with respect for the *whole* person—body, mind, and spirit. I can think of no better voices to guide us through this chapter as we consider how tending to our inner life prepares us to finish strong and to finish well.

———

In the later stages of life, it's common to look back on fond memories. I find myself looking back now more than ever, often spending evening time browsing through old photos, reflecting on the preciousness of small moments, and recalling the stories that have been told throughout the years. Sometimes they make me long for one more taste of the past. Sometimes, their collective beauty just makes me grateful.

As we reflect and remember, what we often see beyond the good are the missed opportunities. Who we wish we could have been and what we wish we had done. Regret doesn't get us anywhere and is too often counterproductive. Yet, there's an important opportunity in the fourth quarter to *become*. It is a time to think about how we'd like to do things differently and make the last quarter of our lives the strongest. Life doesn't change unless we change. The fourth quarter is a chance to find a greater degree of freedom from the hindrances that have held us back all these years.

Some people set themselves up for failure in the fourth quarter by not recognizing that the very things that brought them success in the first three quarters may now work against them. The fourth quarter often requires something different. It calls them to adapt and adjust, even if they've grown comfortable with who they are.

As you step into this chapter, be ready to let go of what's comfortable in order to have an emotionally healthy fourth quarter. You'll be challenged to rethink your perspective on emotional health, the emotional characteristics you'll need, and what stands in the way of your emotional strength. If you are willing to keep learning about your inner world and to lead yourself, your fourth quarter can be filled with more joy, fulfillment, resilience, and high character, even in the midst of changes that accompany aging.

CONSIDER WHAT'S REQUIRED
IN THESE SCENARIOS:

- If your value was based on professional success, what happens to your sense of worth in retirement?
- If you've thrived on being needed as a parent, what is your purpose now that your kids are independent and building their own lives?
- If the unexpected happens, how will you feel safe in the world when you can no longer rely on the predictable path you've known?

By this point in life, you may think, *I am who I am by now. Better just accept it.* But that's only true if you settle. In the book *Falling Upward*, Richard Rohr describes the first half of life as the opportunity to build our identities and establish ourselves. In the second half of life, he suggests that we leverage our challenges and experiences to look inward and grow.

You've never had more capacity for change than you do now, primed with enough life experience to truly understand yourself, maybe for the first time. Ask yourself what isn't working for you to the degree you wish it were. Emotional health isn't a destination you reach as you hit the peak of your lives. It is a continual pursuit until your final breath.

Emotional health isn't a destination we reach as we hit the peak of our lives. It is a continual pursuit until our final breath.

That may sound like unwelcome news. You may hope to coast in later life, relying on the idea of doing less work on yourself, or the thought that you're already emotionally healthy. While emotional health in later life is influenced by how you've lived *to* this point, it's also determined by how you live *from* this point. Key lessons can be carried with you, yet, for most, the fourth quarter still requires a teachable spirit. The world around you will still be changing and will require something of you that life didn't before—perhaps an even greater amount of flexibility, contentment, and security *in who you are* than ever before.

What is your idea of finishing well? Think about that for a moment. Have you considered that it might consist of being a better version of yourself at the end of your life than you were in the beginning?

The fourth quarter of life is not a time to *decline* but a time to *refine*. Emotional health matters at every stage of life, yet there's a unique demand for it in the final quarter. There's also a unique opportunity for it. In our final chapter of life, it's not the time to settle into who we think we are and coast through our remaining days. It's a time to lead beyond past hindrances, to guide our steps toward peace and resilience through change, and to bring out the best within ourselves.

> *The fourth quarter of life is not a time to* decline *but a time to* refine.

WHAT IS EMOTIONAL HEALTH?

Emotional health isn't getting *life* to feel whole or at peace; it's finding wholeness and peace *within*. Key markers of emotional health are:

- Comfort in your authentic self
- Feeling secure and safe in the world
- Experiencing hope, joy, and love even when circumstances are hard
- Capacity to see and believe in what is good
- A soft heart toward others
- Contentment
- Flexibility
- Healthy and hopeful thoughts
- Capacity for connection and trust
- Desire for engagement, pursuit, and purpose
- Internal resilience
- High character

In contrast, emotional unhealthiness is living with an unsettled soul, troubled heart, and burdened mind. Key markers of emotional unhealthiness are:

- Insecurity in who you are
- Feeling unsafe and under threat
- Experiencing despair, hopelessness, anger, or apathy
- Negative and skeptical lens or perspective
- A hardened heart toward others
- Perpetual discontentment
- Rigidity and the need for constant control
- Dark, troubled, or anxious thoughts
- Guardedness against others
- Desire to withdraw, settle, and give up
- Feeling overwhelmed constantly
- Compromised character

Step into an emotionally healthy fourth quarter, or don't. This is not about who has been dealt the right cards; it's about what you do with what you've been given.

> *This is not about who has been dealt the right cards; it's about what you do with what you've been given.*

There's a pathway before you that's offering a way to become a better version of yourself than you were at the beginning. It isn't made up of a series of steps to follow, but it's the way you live your life! You can step on the pathway by examining yourself, adjusting, and investing well. Let's pursue this together—beginning on the path toward greater emotional health in your fourth quarter.

UNDERSTANDING EMOTIONAL HINDRANCES

Without understanding why you do what you do, self-sabotage is inevitable. You'll keep living out the unwanted patterns of the past: perhaps being selfish when you want to be selfless, being too stubborn when you need to ask for help, letting irritability keep love from leading, or pushing people away when all you really want is connection.

If you want to become a better version of yourself than you were before, and live your final chapter from a place of wholeness, *you have to become curious* about the hindrances within you that hold you back. The only way to really change who you are is to change the "why" behind them.

There is power in understanding your past, even as an older adult. After decades have passed, it may not seem like what happened in your childhood or other formative years matters anymore. It can feel like a part of a different life, or as if those experiences belong to someone you no longer recognize. Yet, they still are part of shaping *why* you are who you are and *why* you do what you do.

Even without having a dramatic or traumatic past, everybody's life has still been imperfect. You have inevitably been taught imperfect lessons (by imperfect people), imperfect relational patterns, and imperfect moments. Don't dismiss your story by calling it boring, uneventful, and not as bad as others. It's worth understanding how the little things you wish you didn't do or feel anymore are still driven by something you learned years ago.

Heart Shapers are the events, moments, people, and influences that shape what's inside you. Maybe a parent you couldn't please instilled in you a sense of inadequacy, or repeated betrayals taught you not to let anyone in too close so that you wouldn't become disappointed. Heart Shapers teach us who we are, how to see the world, and how to participate in it. Our early experiences in life still show up in us as adults, even older adults. Time doesn't eventually erase their impact. Only healing does.

Heart Shapers are the events, moments, people,
and influences that shape what's inside you.

These three impacts, among others, often play a key role in shaping our emotional health:

1. *Everyday life experiences* – Small moments that were seemingly insignificant but accumulated into something impactful.

   Examples: Being ignored, creating a sense of rejection; not fitting in at school, creating insecurity; moving frequently, leading to becoming an *adapter or adopter* who fits the environment; being picked on, creating a desire to prove yourself.

2. *Family of origin* – Our primary relationships come from our family and primary caregivers. These relationships are pivotal in shaping how we relate to others, develop our sense of self, and model how to participate in the world.

   Examples: Being overly praised for everything you do, creating pride; being held to an unachievable standard, creating perfectionism; being raised in a home with violence, creating fear; experiencing emotional manipulation, creating a need to appease others.

3. *Defining moments of our lives* – The peaks and valleys of our lives that change things in an instant

   Examples: The death of a caregiver that led to becoming self-reliant; an unexpected tragedy that created anxiety; a significant failure that created inadequacy

Take a moment to reflect:

- What imperfect Heart Shapers are in your story?
- What did they teach you? Did they sow health, security, trust, and hope inside you? Or, instead, did they leave you feeling unimportant, ashamed, unvalued, forgotten, afraid, unprotected, or inadequate?

- How did you learn to live because of the lessons your Heart Shapers taught you?
- How might they still impact you now, even decades later in life?

What do you notice? Don't brush over your story, make excuses for the past, or be afraid of naming reality. While your Heart Shapers may have made many healthy and helpful contributions, their imperfect aspects have power—often too much power—that can become a catalyst for how you live your life.

Heart Shapers leave a mark inside that's called a *Sore Spot*. Sore Spots are the parts of you that have been bruised and beaten up by life, leaving pain and a desire to protect yourself from more.

Sore spots can be:

- Shame
- Pride
- Insecurity
- Inadequacy
- Fear

- Rejection
- Lack of value
- Abandonment
- Unprotectedness
- Anger

Sore Spots often get created early in life and can be reinforced by ongoing experiences. As life goes on, things keep hitting those Sore Spots inside.

- When someone questions your character, it hits the pride in your heart. It sends you instantly into self-defense mode, trying to refute any threat to your ego.
- When your spouse tells you they aren't feeling as loved as they want to be by you, it hits the insecurity in your heart.

You respond with self-condemnation, rehearsing in your mind all the ways you've failed your spouse over the years.

- You get news that someone you love is injured, and it hits the fear in your heart. You start scrambling for any morsel of control you can find to help and make things okay.

Sore Spots don't just create negative feelings; they also influence who we are and how we behave in the world. Without even knowing it, Sore Spots are guiding what we think, what we say, and how we act.

PATTERNS AND IMPACTS

The past patterns and impacts of our lives are present in our lives today in several ways:

- *We draw conclusions based on limited and biased information.*

  As we go through daily life, we are constantly creating meaning out of things. What does this say about me? What does this tell me about you? What does this indicate about the world? If we aren't aware of the unresolved pain we carry, we risk misinterpreting things.

  Here's an example: If you don't get an expected promotion at work, the inadequacy inside you might tell you, *I am incapable of succeeding.* At this point, you can't see objectively, and you dismiss the reality that the boss wasn't playing fair and gave the promotion to their favorite employee. You are not able to experience this as a reflection of the boss's poor leadership, but rather internalize it as a personal failure.

- ***We're enslaved to untrustworthy emotions.***

  How many times have you heard someone say, "Calm down! You are really overreacting!" The moment something touches our place of historical pain, we can go into negative emotional overload. Our feelings take over, shutting out reason and self-control. We can become flooded with feelings that lead us to overrespond or underrespond—by exploding or withdrawing. The response in either case isn't fitting to the moment because it's either too much or too little. That's because our hearts aren't responding to the moment alone, but also to the accumulated experiences and pain inside us.

- ***We're enslaved to faulty solutions.***

  We are often driven by self-protection instead of wisdom when we're carrying unresolved pain. In the example earlier, if your thought after not receiving a promotion is, *I am incapable of succeeding*, you will act accordingly. You might behave as if you aren't a good or capable leader by invalidating your skills and deferring to others in the workplace.

  We try to make the uncomfortable feelings or perceptions go away, usually in unhelpful ways. Without thinking, our self-protective autopilot kicks in, sending us down one of these three routes:

1. ***I have to fix this:*** We desperately want to do something to change the reality of what we're negatively feeling or thinking. When fearing rejection, we might compromise our values or boundaries to keep the other person happy enough to stay in the relationship. When fear is triggered, we may self-produce all the worst-case scenarios, then make a plan to be ready for anything that might come.

2. ***I have to make this go away:*** We try all kinds of ways not to feel or think about what's uncomfortable anymore. We try denial, we compartmentalize—tucking it into an untouched corner of our minds—or we numb our feelings and become anesthetized.

3. ***I have to surrender to this:*** Sometimes we give in to or settle into the pain. For example, when shame rises up, we participate by beating ourselves up and dwelling on our mistakes. When we feel unvalued by others, we withdraw from relationships, convinced that we are wasting others' time and doing them a favor.

The impact of your unresolved past and pain is what drives you to do what you don't want to do. If you aren't careful, self-protection will choose your path. Self-protection becomes your hindrance to joy, peace, and high character. That doesn't bring out the best in you—it's the opposite of being emotionally healthy.

Unresolved pain makes life too much about self. You can be driven by what feels safe or easy rather than by what's loving, by what feels justifying to your ego rather than by what's fair. You can defend more than listen. But when you understand what's inside you, you can begin to lead yourself differently and be driven by something *other* than your past. You can be free to make an impact through helping others, experiencing meaningful moments, or being faithful to work through the hard parts of relationships.

FACING THE PAST AND HEALING

Joseph (not his real name) was an all-around good guy. He had a career that, like so many of us, had its ups and downs. He served in the military, and he found a home there. It seemed as though the military fit who he was, and life made sense there. Then something happened that made no sense: Joseph found out that his mother wasn't really his mother. This discovery, coming in his adult life, was disorienting yet clarifying at the same time. It happened on a trip back to his hometown, a place he hadn't been to in years. Conversations began with old friends and extended to the parents of old friends. Through those conversations, he heard something that he never would have dreamed: The woman he'd identified as his mother was actually a substitute.

This discovery explained an awful lot. He grew up feeling as though he was never really wanted. He grew up with anger that was all around him and often directed *at* him. He grew up feeling like he wasn't good enough, for some reason that had been a mystery to him until that point. While he didn't realize it in his early years, anger wasn't only around him but was inside him too. Anger was Joseph's response to not feeling wanted in his family.

When Joseph went into the military, he loved the structure, including the clear knowledge of how tasks were to be done. He knew exactly how to do things right, and by doing so, he was affirmed, accepted, and regarded in ways he was desperate to be. He loved the camaraderie of "brothers in arms." His combat unit became a family who wanted him, and he wanted them.

However, throughout his career in the military, seemingly inexplicable anger would erupt out of nowhere, exceeding the circumstances by far. He didn't understand his responses and even justified them. The anger came to a head at the end of his career when the unthinkable happened again. He was a senior officer and had been promoted to the coveted position of colonel, yet the date of his promotion fell one day after his military retirement, and he missed out on all the benefits the new title would have brought. To Joseph, that timing appeared intentionally set against him. It seemed like his military family had betrayed him. He couldn't connect the dots to see this at the time, but it was another big betrayal, just like his mother's.

Life went on with unmanaged anger spilling over too often. By age seventy, his wife of forty-six years decided she had had enough. The buried anger and periodic eruptions had taken their toll. He'd never thought she would leave, and when she did, he was enraged. His lifetime of emotional wounds had never been faced or resolved, yet he had never developed any self-awareness. Those wounds deeply impacted his relationships with his wife, kids, and his "brothers in arms." He never broke the unhealthy pattern of anger.

What would it have been like for Joseph if he had become curious about his anger and where it came from? What would it have been like if he'd let someone speak into his life? What difference would it have made if he'd learned the art of self-exploration and self-management? What if he'd asked himself the questions, *How have the patterns I've learned in life destroyed the very relationship I thought I could always count on?* or *How did the painful end of my military career reflect the unresolved pain of my youth?*

Here are the key points about Joseph's story:

- Unresolved hurts often repeat themselves.
- Old wounds often resurface outside of awareness, yet have a powerful impact.
- Just because you deny the wounding in your life doesn't mean it doesn't exist.
- Some of our emotional wounds are obvious, but others take a little more work to unearth and understand.

If life isn't or hasn't been quite what you've expected, perhaps you've got emotional hindrances that haven't been dealt with.

If life isn't or hasn't been quite what you've expected, perhaps you've got emotional hindrances that haven't been dealt with.

Pain has sculpted you in positive ways in certain aspects of your life. Maybe you've learned to make better choices or how to be wise with how you give away trust. But you might also find that pain has led you to a place of self-protection instead of freedom, taught you to settle as if this is as good as it gets, or encouraged you to give in to feeling helpless and hopeless—as if the fourth quarter is not a time of opportunity but a time to wait out the inevitable.

You might discover that your inner world is more complex than you realized. So many things wind up having an impact, and you might not fully understand what that impact is unless you're being intentional to both identify and understand it.

If you want to understand yourself, take time in solitude to ask questions. Adopt a new sense of curiosity about yourself and record those reflections in a journal. Challenge yourself to be more vulnerable and honest than you've ever been as you explore the uncomfortable places and times of your past.

Think about these questions:

- How has my past shaped me?
- How are my emotions today influenced by the experiences of my past?
- What did I learn about who I am from the way I was loved and related to?
- How are my expectations of others a product of what my past relationships looked like?
- How are my life strategies built to protect me from being hurt or disappointed?

- What did I have the best intentions of doing or being that I didn't execute well?
- What has kept me doing the same thing over and over again and expecting a different outcome? (We've all heard that one before. It's Einstein's definition of insanity.)
- What has been dragging me down to a version of myself I don't like?
- How do I talk to myself in ways that others who care about me wouldn't agree with?

What can you do with your new self-understanding? Begin by identifying what life would look like without your hindrances. Create small yet meaningful challenges to move you one step closer to this life at a time. Consider participating in counseling to guide healing from what is holding you back.

Seeking Feedback

Sometimes we see a limited picture of ourselves. The best way to know yourself is to see yourself through the eyes of trustworthy others. There are two things we want to better understand through feedback.

1. **Blind spots:** The first is your *blind spots*. Your normal is only normal to you. What you think and what you do are often instinctual by this stage of life. Someone else can help you see what you can't see regarding how you present yourself, and see what that might say about the pain you are carrying or your unhealthy thoughts.

2. **Impact:** The second piece to understand is your *impact*. You simply can't know your impact on others unless you ask those you influence. How do you come across to others? How do others feel when they interact with you? How do your words

or moods affect others? Do others receive what you intend to say?

It can be an intimidating step to ask someone for feedback about yourself. What if they reveal something about you that you don't want to hear? The risk isn't in the feedback; *it's in letting it defeat you.* Feedback is an opportunity to grow. Become curious about why you do what you do so you can remove the hindrances that keep you stuck in that way of being, and strengthen a relationship by learning to present yourself differently. Let people who know you well tell you the truth by holding up the mirror for you. This growth potential is led by a choice to become all you can be in the fourth quarter of living. It's an investment that can yield high dividends!

Invite five people to give you feedback on questions like these:

- How do you experience me?
- Which three words best describe who I am, not what I do?
- What emotions do I display most often?
- What do you notice about the way I see the world?
- What do you notice about the way I interact with others?
- How do you think I see myself?
- From the stories I've told you, what do you think might still impact me from my past?
- Where do you see me stuck or hitting the same barrier?

When you get the feedback, your job is to deeply consider it. That means treating it as something that could be true. Watch your defensiveness. Don't reject it without examination because you can't risk a hit to your pride. Emotionally healthy people are humbly secure.

The pathway to emotional health is journeyed as you invite trusted others to speak into your life and illuminate for you that which you can't see for yourself.

LOOKING BACK TO LOOK FORWARD

The windshield is bigger than the rearview mirror for a reason—to have our eyes fixed forward rather than stuck on the mistakes or troubles of the past. Yet, looking back helps us move forward well. In the fourth quarter, we need to interpret our past through a lens that leads to growth and wholeness.

By the fourth quarter, there's ample history in the rearview mirror. Hopefully, you have a plethora of cherished memories. But, more than likely, you've also accumulated your fair share of disappointments and regrets, such as things left unsaid or undone. The worst part is the hindsight and knowing what you know now that you didn't know then. Regrets and disappointments can come with self-judgment and the thought: *It shouldn't have been the way it was.* So how do you not live in regret?

An important task of the fourth quarter is to reflect back on your life story to find the meaning and purpose in it, no matter the outcome. How did what happened then lead you to where you are now? That question doesn't minimize the realities of missed opportunities, unruly behavior, or the consequences of them. Yet, it sees beyond them into the bigger picture. Leading an examined life is not only about probing each moment as it comes, but also about inspecting the whole to connect the dots. Perspective and acceptance come when you begin to appreciate how even mistakes and unmet expectations may have propelled you forward.

Perspective and acceptance come when you begin to appreciate how even mistakes and unmet expectations may have propelled you forward.

Make a Timeline

- ***Mark the lows:*** Mark "low" on the moments of regret, disappointment, pain, and hurt throughout your life.
- ***Mark the highs:*** Mark "high" on cherished moments of growth, success, or joy.
- ***Trace it back:*** For each high moment, look back to see what events or choices led you there.
- ***See the whole:*** Notice how the highs and lows are connected rather than random. See your life as a journey shaped by both joys and trials.
- ***Reflect:*** Write in your journal about how the dots connect in your life—what helpful purpose have the highs and lows played in shaping how you live life today?

If that exercise proves more discouraging than encouraging, it might be telling you that you haven't learned or grown yet because of your missteps. So let them propel you now! Learn the lessons you need to absorb. Make amends and forgive yourself so you can live by grace and at peace with others. Through mentorship, you can leverage the pain you experienced to bless someone now who is in your old shoes.

The point of self-reflection is not about becoming self-absorbed but gaining self-insight. That's the ticket to freedom—choosing a new trajectory. You don't have to abandon all the lessons you learned in the past, but you do need to evaluate them to see if they are worth preserving.

It's not too late to face your past. It's not too late to understand yourself. It's time to leverage the fourth quarter as a chance to heal and redeem what's been holding you back.

THE POWER OF SELF-LEADERSHIP IN EMOTIONAL HEALTH

The only real thing you have control over in your life is yourself. When you face yourself, there becomes so much possibility for who you *can* be, no matter who you've been up to this point. You have proclivities and decades of deeply ingrained habits to discipline, like everyone on earth, and it takes self-leadership and the desire to change and to live differently to be whole. Most importantly, your true self can lead rather than your wounded self. As we gently guide our hearts to wholeness and resilience in the fourth quarter, there's a pathway of self-leadership to follow that can lead to healing, growth, and adaptation. It's not made up of steps, but of guiding principles.

- *Be aware*: As something becomes uncomfortable, become curious. Ask yourself what it is bringing up in you. Acknowledge what you are feeling, thinking, and needing, and evaluate whether it is healthy.
- *Be in charge*: Name the new targets of what you want to pursue, change, or build as you move forward. Guide your heart beyond its instincts. Break loyalty to your "normal." Regulate your emotions that can mislead you. Challenge your thinking and your behavior to align with wisdom over self-protection.
- *Be in reflection:* Spend time on a regular or daily basis to examine what's in you and what's coming out of you. Think

about your recent patterns of thinking. What kinds of thoughts have been in your mind lately? Which of those needs to be disciplined to the truth and not your perception?

Think about your recent patterns of emotions. What emotions are emerging from you? Which of those are guiding you well, and which need to be faced and redeemed? Think about the way you are behaving lately. Are the strategies you're using (responses and behaviors) blessing the world or protecting and indulging you? Use this reflection time to notice, learn, heal, and adjust.

You learn things like resilience (the ability to keep going when things get hard); forged humility (learning to put others before yourself); patient endurance (the ability to withstand discomfort); and steadfast love (unconditional regard and care for others) by leading yourself beyond your normal. This might seem daunting, but take courage. Just start the process one piece at a time.

Continue any practice you currently have that leads you into reflection and challenges you forward. Yet don't stop there. Lead yourself into experiences that take you out of your norm, providing fresh ways to receive and learn. Consider trying something from the following list:

Encountering nature: As you enjoy nature, look for ways to harness more of what you see. Perhaps it's the peace you find in the quiet forest, the power you hear in the ocean waves, the intentional living you see in animals' food collection, or the gentleness you feel from the breeze on your skin. Sit with an example you see and imagine it being within you.

Reading: Select books that speak to the parts of you that you want to see transformed—a book on forgiveness or grace as you wrestle through accepting yourself through your mistakes and regrets, or a book on trust as you lay down your anxieties toward the future. Don't read for the sake of knowing; read for the sake of receiving.

> *Don't read for the sake of knowing; read for the sake of receiving.*

Restorative solitude: In the quiet stillness, be present to what is within you. Take inventory of your thoughts and feelings. Notice what they tell you. Use mindfulness practices to center yourself and find peace within.

Exercise and movement: Find release and energy through physical movement. Let your mind and heart be clear and become receptive.

Encouraging fellowship: Allow others to speak into your life. Let corrective experiences of being loved, cared for, valued, believed in, or encouraged heal you. Let others encourage you in the path you choose.

Creative expression: Allow yourself to explore your own thoughts, emotions, and hidden world within as you write, paint, draw, sing, or build something new. Use creative mediums to develop experiential reminders of who you are becoming.

Serving: Volunteer and help in ways that allow you to practice being who you are becoming. If you want to find purpose, join a serving team through your community or church. If you want to feel like a difference maker, use your skills in a fresh way within your new capacity.

Learning: Put yourself in intentional positions to learn something new. Take a class. Sit with a mentor (yes, even at this age!). Study and read. Practice a new skill.

Although self-leadership is key, you don't have to do this on your own. Invite a counselor in (yes, even at this age!). Engage a faith community as a way to find a new perspective, or let faith be a part of your healing. Learn from those who have gone before you and ask others how they've worked through the things of their past.

Self-leadership requires you to break your norm and do something different. Don't settle in the fourth quarter. Step up, keep going, and lead yourself well.

NAVIGATING SHIFTS IN THE FOURTH QUARTER

The last quarter of life can take you on an emotional ride. It may appear as a simpler time of life at first glance—perhaps a chance to scale back professionally or fully retire with fewer schedule demands and the chance for more freedom to simply do what's desired. It can also be an exciting time—a chance to dream new dreams and fulfill the dreams you've carried for a lifetime. In any case, the fourth quarter offers increased opportunity for richer relationships and for reflection and growth.

It can also be a weighty time, and even a disorienting one. For many, the greatest challenges come when the unexpected arrives and life throws a curveball.

Jane and Mark

Jane and Mark were a couple who didn't see that coming in their fourth quarter.

In order to appreciate the impact of the unexpected things that came into their lives, it is important to understand the story behind them.

Jane built her identity on being independent and able to manage anything. She was a farm girl who grew up helping to carry the weight. She went on to become a successful attorney, the first female in her division. She never had to worry about limitations and was able to do whatever she set her mind to. After thirteen breaks and fractures in fifteen years, she was diagnosed with osteoporosis. Now in her fifties, she didn't see that one coming. The farm girl who started her day at 4:00 a.m. and was capable of anything now needed help. She had to learn to live differently—be constantly mindful of trip hazards to avoid another break, let others do tasks she used to do for herself, and accept the look of confusion and rejection on her young grandson's face when she told him she couldn't pick him up anymore. This life of limitations wasn't one she was used to, nor one that felt good.

Jane didn't like asking for help, but she had to learn that this wasn't a weakness. She didn't like feeling as if she was letting anyone down, especially her grandson, but she had to trust that her need for help did not lessen how she showed love. She didn't like feeling vulnerable and weak, yet had to learn that it didn't threaten her identity and value. She faced her fear of being needy and found hope in a future that might look different than what she'd expected.

Jane's husband, Mark, got a cancer diagnosis before he was ready to let go of his career. Cancer wasn't his choice, but it was real. Surgery removed the cancerous tumor, giving him a healthy prognosis for his future, but the lasting consequences of cancer meant that Mark didn't come back the same. He didn't trust his thinking like he used to, leaving him questioning his professional abilities as a counselor. The physical changes to his body kept him more homebound than he would have liked and prevented him from traveling, even to see his daughter. He could no longer eat the foods he cooked that had once been his chief way of showing love through hospitality. Mark felt like he had to stop before reaching the finish he once imagined, falling short of the purpose and capacity he thought he'd still have to contribute.

Mark had to grieve the unexpected and what was lost, but once he did, he was able to begin *reimagining*. Rather than expect the same from himself, his life took a new format, and he began using his gifts to serve in new ways: mentoring the next generation, leveraging the moments of energy to write in short bursts, and finding creative ways to serve his family and neighbors with what he *could* give. Mark figured out that joy could be found beyond his limitations. He disciplined his thoughts when they wandered to what could have been, recognizing the indulgence of them as a highway to frustration and hopelessness. Instead, he challenged himself to be content in all circumstances, focusing every day on simple beauties within. One final lesson Mark learned was to bring a little humor as he faced his limitations, which added a sense of lightness and helped him accept the difficulty and shame he was carrying.

- A good day can come disguised as a really bad day.
- Expectations impede us more than our limits.
- Sometimes we need to grieve before we can appreciate.
- A little humor can help us keep a healthy perspective.
- Joy and beauty are found in simplicity too.
- Facing fears opens up the chance for good to be found.

You might be prepared financially yet still face a curveball when you lose your spouse earlier than expected. You might be prepared with a new purpose for retirement yet not be prepared for the loss of influence you still feel. You might be prepared to finish well in your career, only to be disappointed with how the new leaders disregard what you've built. You might have ideas about the fun you'll have, only to find out you don't have the energy you thought you would. And it's possible that you won't have as much control as you probably want to have over what happens and when it happens.

So, ask yourself how you typically react in times of pain and ambiguity. That may take some time to answer. Pausing now to consider this question will help you process as you proceed through this chapter.

Most of us don't think we are controlling until control is taken away. The desire for it is revealed when the unknown hits, and our response is marked by the frenzy of pressure, worry, anger, and guilt that comes with not being able to live up to the list of should-haves we've created for ourselves. Sometimes we're annoyed and irritated about what used to work but doesn't seem to be working now, even if we can't put the process into words.

At some point, we have to come to grips with our humanity. We are not completely in control of the outcomes of our lives, and we're not supposed to be. The famous serenity prayer: "God, grant me the serenity to accept the things I cannot change, courage to change the things I can, and wisdom to know the difference" confirms this.[1]

---

[1] The Serenity Prayer is most commonly attributed to Reinhold Niebuhr (1892–1971), a prominent American theologian, ethicist, and pastor. However, its exact origins are debated, with some evidence suggesting earlier versions existed in oral traditions or unpublished works. Niebuhr's version gained prominence through its adoption by Alcoholics Anonymous in the 1940s. Reinhold Niebuhr's original version, as documented in early sources like a 1934 sermon, is slightly longer and worded differently in some contexts. For example, one

To untether our well-being from how well things are going, we have to be able to hope and trust in something beyond them. We need something that is stable when life isn't. Some examples of that are:

- My internal value is secure and unchangeable, no matter how the world values me.
- Hope can always lie ahead of where I am right now.
- There is still goodness in humanity, even though others are broken and flawed.

Emotionally healthy people are flexible and adapt to what comes. It doesn't mean the grieving that change brings is any easier. It just means that you don't see ambiguity as an enemy, and you adjust your expectations.

The goal is to trade expectations for expectancy, the difference being that expectations come with a predicted outcome. Expectancy is the anticipation of good without a defined way to get there. Expectancy is less prescriptive, less rigid, and leaves room for the unexpected.

Expectancy doesn't mean you can't dream. It just means you need to remain open-handed and preserve the anticipation of good if you have to shift the route. That can feel like an incredible, and even cruel, challenge when you're dealing with something significant like a chronic illness or losing someone you love. Although the difficulty is still hard, purpose, growth, and unexpected blessings can live within hardship, loss, and the unexpected too. Pain can be a strategic part of maturing and growing us, even in our later years—if we let it.

An expectant outlook on the future comes free of judgment. Sometimes you need a new outlook on yourself that reflects ac-

---

early version reads: "Father, give us courage to change what must be altered, serenity to accept what cannot be helped, and the insight to know the one from the other."

ceptance of changes to your body, to your relationship status, or to your limitations. Sometimes you need a new hope in life to find contentment in *what is*, rather than what you'd dreamed *would be*. For those with faith, your view of God may need to be redefined in order to trust him when unexpected loss or conflict disrupts your world. Expectancy makes room for your current reality and breeds acceptance, contentment, and maybe even joy in a life that won't always go according to plan.

> *Expectancy makes room for your current reality and breeds acceptance, contentment, and maybe even joy in a life that won't always go according to plan.*

One of the greatest dangers of the fourth quarter is being immovable—not letting go of what you expected and demanding control in a life that doesn't always submit to that. Don't try to make the fourth quarter fit the model of the first three. Don't let your hope be stolen by circumstances you can't control. Emotional health is found in being able to separate your well-being from whether today went according to plan or not.

The reality is that life doesn't stop being difficult, even in the golden years. The target is not to make life less difficult but to learn to live well in a different and sometimes tough world.

CHANGING RELATIONSHIPS

CONSIDER THESE EXPERIENCES:

- "What I least expected was to feel like I didn't fit anywhere." —Early retiree who didn't fit with the older crowd that matched her stage of life, nor did she fit with her age group, who were still engaged in careers.
- "The hardest thing for me is my shrinking community." —A snowbird who thought the winters away wouldn't change her connections when she came back home.
- "What makes me feel the most unvalued was feeling like a nuisance to my adult kids, who seem too busy for me." —A father whose expectations of family weren't met.

Relationships change frequently throughout a lifetime, yet the fourth quarter can sometimes bring an onslaught of relational changes, sometimes overnight.

Children are no longer children and have their own lives to live. You have to learn new ways of relating to them and finding your place in their world. Marriage takes center stage when the children move out, but what is that like after a lifetime of focusing on everyone but each other? Longtime friends might drift away, and work relationships often fade as careers wind down. What does it feel like when your relational circles shrink or change?

Relational health in the fourth quarter is fully addressed in chapter 2, and you can reference those pages for a richer dive into building healthy connections and relational fulfillment. Yet, for now, notice the tie between relational changes and your emotional health.

While change is inevitable, you're getting the point through this chapter that opportunity is too. To guard against isolation, feeling unvalued or unseen, or being left in an echo chamber, it's critical that you stay in pursuit of healthy community in your fourth quarter. Even if you've had bad experiences so far and think a life with fewer people sounds best, *trust that a healthy community is out there.* It's a key to emotional health.

If you need to find new ways to connect, try serving or volunteering. Find the courage to go meet neighbors you've lived next to for years but have never really known. Work on relationships that don't have to fall away with life changes.

Emotionally healthy people grow through the wisdom, challenges, healing opportunities, encouragement, and learning that are found in relationships.

Dreaming New Dreams

Sometimes dreams end and won't follow you into the fourth quarter. Sometimes your fourth quarter plan isn't all it's cracked up to be. Now what?

You might need to dream new dreams. Don't be afraid of that. Many of us spend our entire lives planned out—we know the track we're on. We know what is supposed to come next. This new freedom of the fourth quarter can feel too nebulous sometimes. We're often trapped by wondering what we are *supposed* to do.

You might need to dream new dreams. Don't be afraid of that.

While you stay true to yourself and your values, you've got to explore and intentionally put yourself in new experiences. Consider these questions:

- What have I always wanted to do that I couldn't?
- What new skill do I want to learn?
- What do I want to enjoy the most in this season of life?
- What have I been too afraid to try or pursue?

Within reason, and with trusted company, take a risk! Stepping outside of your norm or comfort zone might not go well the first time. Don't let that defeat you. Try one more time, just in case there's a surprise waiting for you. You might not know what you are capable of until your heart and mind have a chance to learn something new.

Audrey

Let's examine Audrey's life as she transitions, unexpectedly, into widowhood and then into surprising growth.

Audrey stepped into the fourth quarter unsure. After losing her husband too early to a heart attack, she felt adrift. That wasn't a new feeling; actually, it was quite familiar. She hadn't historically been a dreamer. She'd spent her life following the trail that life led her on. And now, with no real direction, her longtime friend could see what she needed: opportunity. He offered her a job to supplement her income and give her something to do. It became so much more than that.

Through the job, Audrey gained confidence and a new direction. She began valuing a skill she never saw value in before—

her gift of relationship building. She could talk to anyone, make anyone feel at ease and feel valued. Within the organization she now worked for, this was an asset to their mission.

As Audrey was stretched—within her skillset, as well as in who she thought she was—she began to turn the question of apprehension about what she would do next into a question of possibility and expectancy. She stopped living by the old lesson—follow where life goes—and began leading her own path. She stopped seeing herself as an "aside" and began seeing herself as a difference maker. As her perceptions changed, so did her experience. Audrey came alive, maybe for the first time.

EMOTIONAL FREEDOM AND THE UNHINDERED LIFE

The fourth quarter holds so much—both the richness of life that comes before and the regrets of life unfulfilled; the opportunities that come with new freedom and the angst of change and loss; the expected blessings and the unexpected challenges that you didn't see coming. The fourth quarter can offer new freedom, but emotional health is required to live and stay there, regardless of your fourth quarter circumstances. There is much to navigate in your internal world in the fourth quarter. If you do that well, you can finish well.

The fourth quarter is an opportunity for transformation and a reinvented self. In other words, it's a chance to live unhindered from all that's held you back. It's time to leverage the lessons you've learned along the way and set the model you want others to follow.

Your emotional health will shape the legacy you leave behind. What impact do you have on the people around you? What does it do to someone when you lash out and say things about their character you don't mean? What is the impact of what doesn't get said when you hold back loving words, or you worry too much about what people think to give them the honest feedback they need? In contrast, what good gets marked on someone's heart when you meet them in their time of need? How do you positively shape someone's identity when you speak life into their gifts and tell them you love them? Your emotional health contributes to the emotional health of others.

Your legacy is also in the lessons you leave behind. Will you show people what it looks like to age with grace? Will you show others how to learn from the mistakes you haven't learned from yet, even in your later years? Will you practice self-management so you can show up with extravagant kindness, generosity, patience, joy, and love? Will you heal the wounds you've never taken the time to face and let that leave a new legacy in your relationships? Will you show others who are a step behind you in life how to navigate the challenges and transitions of the fourth quarter with intentionality and hope?

One of the best examples I have of intentional and unhindered living comes from a friend of mine who passed away recently. He never slowed down, even into his final year at age seventy-eight. After leaving his forty-year career in business at age sixty-three, he launched a nonprofit organization to create soul-enriching leadership cohorts. It wasn't about wanting to be busy. It was about wanting to be a difference maker. He died on a mission.

At his memorial service, each person who spoke described him as someone who'd left a blessing in his wake—how he left others better than he found them, how he asked curious questions that challenged assumptions, and famously asked, over and over, "How hard can it be?" when faced with a challenge.

In his quarterly writings, he shared about what he was learning—about himself and the world—and what he was grateful for. His written insights made others better. He used relational strength to protect the character to which he was so committed. He died a man with a legacy of integrity, wisdom, character, purpose, and life. His fourth quarter became the most meaningful chapter of his life.

My friend's story lights a fire in me. I hope it does in you too. As you continue to process through life with self-examination and input from trusted friends and family members, changing what needs to change, exploring new horizons for the fourth quarter, and believing you are capable of each, my encouragement to you is this: Stay in pursuit of your emotional health because it's not time to coast, it's time to become! Your legacy is still being written, and you are the author. You have the ability to author what you want others to read, so be authentic and be whole!

Your legacy is still being written,
and you are the author.

CHAPTER 2

RELATIONALLY RICH

By Pastor Rick Craig

Have you ever reached a point in life when you stopped and asked yourself what really matters? Clarity might have suddenly hit you during a hardship, a moment of success, or maybe even during an ordinary day. I had one of those moments when I realized I was in the fourth quarter of my life—a time when every decision, every relationship, and every value mattered more than ever.

Each season of life brings unique opportunities. What I call "fourth quarter living" offers a season to be intentional. It isn't solely about aging; it's also about living with wisdom, purpose, and gratitude. It becomes essential to nurture meaningful relationships that reflect our values, provide support, and offer contributions to our lasting legacy.

What would happen if you audited toxic, challenging, or high-maintenance relationships in your life? Would it reveal changes that need to be made? If you have relationships that are one-sided, where you are providing energy and health only to have them consumed time after time, have you asked yourself why there's such an imbalance of investment by the other party?

Are your closest friends people you truly admire, with virtues you aspire to have? Are you benefiting from their input, and do you trust them enough to be in your inner circle? Do you have an inner circle of friends? If so, who are they? We'll dive deeper into this topic later in this chapter.

Relationships are among life's greatest treasures, and like any treasure, how we tend them determines their lasting value. You might think of them as investments—investments of time, love, and care—that can yield either positive or negative returns. A wise relational investment—like a financial one—should grow in value and provide increasing returns over time. I invite you to join me as I share what I've learned over decades of building and nurturing healthy relationships. At the end of this chapter, I will challenge you to reflect on your relationships with the same care you'd give to an audit because in the fourth quarter of life, you want your investments to bring the highest yield.

In this chapter, we'll explore eleven virtues that shape a meaningful life, and how embracing them can transform our relationships, decisions, and legacy. These virtues are honesty, humility, patience, kindness, forgiveness, gratitude, perseverance, empathy, generosity, courage, and self-control.

My hope is that this chapter on being relationally rich will help you recognize and prioritize healthy connections that truly matter.

CHILDHOOD FRIENDSHIPS

I grew up in the farming community of Woodstock, Ontario, during the late 1950s and early '60s. In those days, life in Canada moved at a slower pace—often a decade or two behind the cultural trends and conveniences of the United States.

In first and second grade, I had a friend named Gunther, whose father had been a German soldier captured during World War II and held as a prisoner of war (POW) near our small town until the war ended. My mum told me that these POWs would escape on occasion, but only to head straight to the pub, hoping to have a cold one. Each and every time, they were apprehended by the authorities and sent back to their temporary home.

At the end of the war, Canada offered amnesty to POWs if they wanted to stay to become farmers and help populate Canada. Since they weren't mistreated as prisoners and were eager to start new lives, many of them stayed, while others went back to rebuild Germany. Gunther's father was among those who chose to stay in Canada. He became a resident farmer, sent for his wife from Germany, and then started a family years later. I recall with fond memories Gunther's laugh and his accent, since his parents spoke primarily German at home. We were bound for a long-term friendship, but it ended abruptly when my parents announced that we were moving to Anaheim, Southern California, for a new life and warmer weather.

My father's damaged knee from playing hockey and fast-pitch softball, along with Canada's brutally cold winters, created unbearable pain for him. Our region lacked the medical expertise to repair his knee properly, so he had submitted to exploratory surgeries in Canada and then in the United States. Both were unsuccessful, and the pain persisted. But the warmer year-round weather in Southern California helped him, as we settled in our new community.

As I entered elementary school, then junior high and high school, I developed friendships that are still strong today. I didn't realize it then, but *fostering* relationships is an investment. For an introvert, this process can be painfully arduous, but it often leads to lasting relationships. Those who intentionally invest in relationships tend to have a larger and more diverse circle of friends. That's been true for me. By intentionally fostering relationships, I have been blessed with a network of friends who are *relationally rich*.

IDENTIFYING VIRTUES

Virtues are the guiding qualities that drive ethical choices and shape decisions leading to meaningful, lasting outcomes. Virtues serve as foundational principles, such as honesty, humility, patience, kindness, forgiveness, gratitude, perseverance, empathy, generosity, courage, self-control, and more. Over the years, I've discovered that a life of wisdom and integrity is built on having core virtues. They not only reveal who we are but also shape the way we impact those around us.

In all quarters of life, fostering and maintaining friendships—especially with your inner circle—requires prioritizing shared virtues that both reflect who you are and who you aspire to become. I'll explain this in greater depth later in this chapter.

ELEVEN VIRTUES OF HEALTHY RELATIONSHIPS

Virtue #1 – Honesty: The Foundation of Trust

When I was eight years old, we lived in a large apartment complex directly across from the Disneyland Hotel in Anaheim, California. When we opened our front door, the first thing we saw was a small nine-hole golf course, and we heard golfers walking, talking, and enjoying their games. The hotel, which was right behind the golf course, had a gift shop filled with memorabilia of Disneyland and trinkets. With Disneyland Hotel so close, and the entire neighborhood filled with kids, we viewed the hotel and the surrounding orange groves and strawberry fields as our playground. Trips to the gift shop for candy—both the eye candy of toys and the real candy filled with sugar—were a weekly experience. I was particularly fond of those little green army men action figures, and they often found their way into my pockets without me paying for them.

One day, when I was playing with my platoon of toy army men, my dad walked into my bedroom and calmly asked, "Where did you get all of these toys?"

My heart began to pound, but thinking quickly, I immediately said, "Dad, as the golfers walk by, I sell them golf balls I find on our side of the fence, and I caddie for them too."
With complete composure, he nodded, said "Alright," and left.

About a week or two later, we were casually talking, and he asked how selling golf balls and caddying for players was coming along.

I told him, "Fine. I've been out selling golf balls just recently."

He responded with a quiet but authoritative voice, "No, you haven't, because your mum and I have been watching, and you have never been out there, so what is the truth?"

I was caught stealing and lying! With love and grace, my dad sat me down and shared the negatives about stealing and lying. He also said, "The Craig family doesn't steal or lie, so now we have to go to the Disneyland gift shop so you can confess, and I will pay for the stolen items."

I apologized profusely, then off we went to the gift store, where I repeated my apology to the store clerk. She accepted my apology, but with a caveat: I was not welcome back! It was a lesson that has stuck with me to this day.

Honesty Attracts

Some character traits attract people, while other traits tend to push people away. Honesty is a trait that attracts. It creates clarity between friends while fostering authenticity. Honesty is the gateway to trust, and it unlocks the heart and mind to see and hear different perspectives. And when honesty and trust prevail, a relationship becomes a safe place to share and receive differing perspectives.

Honesty vs. Integrity

Integrity is a virtue that differs from honesty yet is complementary to it. While honesty is speaking and acting truthfully, admitting mistakes, avoiding exaggeration, and being trustworthy, *integrity is about wholeness of character.* When comparing the two, honesty is what you do or say when confronted, while integrity is doing the right thing even when nobody is watching or listening. Honesty is telling the truth, while integrity is living the truth.

> *Honesty is telling the truth, while integrity is living the truth.*

My dad acted with integrity when he confronted me about stealing, then made things right by taking me to the gift shop so I could confess my stealing while he paid for the merchandise. He didn't have to take this course of action, but he was a man of integrity, and his actions proved that.

What honesty looks like	What a lack of honesty looks like
Telling the truth, even in difficult circumstances	Avoiding the truth Lying or telling a partial truth Embellishment
Admitting mistakes	Covering up mistakes Blaming someone else Lying Omission
Speaking the truth in love	Avoidance Partial truth A lack of transparency A lack of compassion
Consistency in character	Untrustworthiness

REFLECTIVE QUESTION

When was the last time you bent the truth—either to protect yourself or someone else? What might have changed if you had chosen complete honesty?

Closing Thought

Honesty is more than telling the truth; it's also about living truthfully, even when it costs you something. In the fourth quarter of life, honesty becomes a legacy virtue. It lays a foundation of trust, credibility, and peace that others can stand on long after you're gone. Live in a way that your words match your actions, whether or not anyone is watching.

Virtue #2 – Humility: Putting Others Before Yourself

I have a friend who served in the United States Coast Guard, and upon his discharge, he trained, graduated, and then went to work for the local fire department as a paramedic. Through his dedication, he moved upward in rank to captain over the course of his career.

Firefighters, paramedics, and other first responders spend countless hours side by side. Out of that time, trust grows, and from trust comes a bond that's hard to describe unless you've lived it. These friendships are rare, and once you have one, you hold onto it. I have a friend like that. We laugh together and share life together. I thought I knew his story. But years into our friendship, I discovered something he had never told me. I knew his military and fire department careers had been about saving lives—that much seemed obvious. What I didn't know was that he also carried the weight of recovering the bodies of those who couldn't be saved. For all those years, he had kept that part of his story to himself. Why had he carried that burden alone?

One of the virtues my friend has, and one that I love about him, is his humility. He could have easily flaunted his importance and value in both careers, signaling his uniqueness and right to be celebrated. But he never has—ever! Instead, he uses his experience to help others without explaining his past because of his humility. He's one of my inner circle of friends. I'll do anything for him, and he for me!

Humility requires setting ego and pride aside. Relationships are not about bragging or control but mutual care and understanding. Like honesty, humility attracts people because it's admirable and it creates a sense of safety in new and long-lasting friendships.

Humility seeks reconciliation in strained relationships and helps prevent grudges by encouraging healthy self-reflection and a willingness to admit mistakes. Humility can open doors to new relationships and sustain existing ones. Pause from your reading and think about your humble friends and the impact they have on your life. What do you appreciate about them? Let them know! Expressing gratitude for their friendship is both encouraging and honoring to them.

What humility looks like	What a lack of humility looks like
Putting others first	Self-centered Selfish
Keeping one's pride in check	Proud Egotistical Overbearing Haughty
Listening to understand	Interrupting A need to be right
Being teachable	Un-coachable Defensive
Celebrating others' successes and achievements	Competitive Comparing Downplaying

REFLECTIVE QUESTION

Think about a time when you insisted on being right or being recognized. What might humility have looked like at that moment?

Closing Thought

Humility isn't a weakness but rather a strength under control. It speaks softly in a world full of noise. As we mature in life, humility becomes a bridge—one that connects generations, restores relationships, and invites others into friendships.

Virtue #3 – Patience: Enduring with Grace

Not long after my mum passed away, my dad was diagnosed with dementia. He moved in with my son and his family to keep him close to what was familiar, and to help him stay connected and comfortable. Eventually, he moved close to me as his dementia progressed, so I could spend time with him and care for him. That's when I realized the impact dementia had on him and what caretakers experience. It's a harsh reality to be with someone you've known for years, but they cannot recall in detail their time with you. It's humbling and heartbreaking!

His move to be closer to me started with finding a residence where he had his freedom, but with watchful eyes and assistance when needed. I visited in the mornings and quite often after work.

Our relationship, which had been nothing but incredible my entire life, began to change as he settled into his new residence. Our relationship became more of me acting as his caretaker—checking that he was taking his pills, bathing, making it to the dining area on time, and attending doctor appointments. During my visits, I found that sitting and talking with him no longer offered the same rich experiences they had in the past. I was losing my patience with the conversational loops dementia creates—hearing the same story over and over—even though my love for him remained unchanged!

In my frustration, a friend of mine made a suggestion, called "throwing out the silver lure!" It's what my dad had taught me about fishing on those warm, sunny summer days as a kid—throwing a lure or bait out for the fish to focus on and "luring them in." Applying that concept to my father, I would gently interrupt him when he was repeating the same story with a question or topic he was familiar with, such as: "How was your golf game yesterday?" He hadn't played in years but was a professional golfer at one time, so he would pick up the conversation and tell me all about it. I would marvel at his recall as he offered imagery of certain fairways and greens, and even his score. When it was time to change topics because the loop had started again, I would throw out another silver lure, and we would engage in a new conversation.

With his declining health and our declining relationship with me as his caretaker, I finally admitted that I needed help and eventually hired someone to care for him. That's when I became his son again, not the caretaker he would push back on, which allowed us to enjoy our conversations. I miss him and our conversations immensely, and I am forever grateful to my son and daughter-in-law for caring for him.

Aging comes with changes in energy levels and physical and mental abilities, along with a great need for patience. Remaining steadfast and empathetic with friends and family throughout life, but especially in the fourth quarter, offers powerful opportunities to express love through patience and forgiveness.

Here is a comparison of patience through grace and patience through conditioning.

Patience through grace	Patience through conditioning
Guided by purpose and values	Driven by goals or external outcomes
Leads to peace, acceptance, and transformation	Leads to restraint and control
Aligns with deep personal and spiritual beliefs	May falter without consistent habit formation
Addresses the heart and soul	Focus on behavior and external actions

What patience looks like	What a lack of patience looks like
Listening contently	Interrupting Easily angered Easily frustrated
Remaining calm in stressful situations	Agitated Impulsive
Offering grace	Interrupting Avoiding
Being empathetic	Sarcasm or indifference

REFLECTIVE QUESTION

Who in your life is testing your patience right now? What might it look like to respond to them with grace instead of frustration? What could happen if you spoke to them honestly about the issue of patience while trying to find common ground on which to grow?

Closing Thought

Patience is not passive—it is active love. Whether rooted in grace or shaped by discipline, patience shows our willingness to value others even when it's difficult. In the fourth quarter, patience becomes a quiet gift we give to those who need *our presence* in each moment more than *our solutions.*

Virtue #4 – Kindness: Love in Action

Caring for one another through acts of love—such as generosity, empathy, compassion, and thoughtfulness—is a strong indicator of a life focused on others rather than self. Kindness is not just about grand gestures; it's also about consistent, intentional actions that make a meaningful difference in the lives of others. Think about the last time you did something kind for someone. Now ask yourself if there was an expectation attached to it. Would you still have done it if they could never repay you? True kindness isn't about reciprocity but rather giving freely, without strings attached. The real test of kindness is in how we treat those who have nothing to offer us in return.

> *True kindness isn't about reciprocity but rather giving freely, without strings attached.*

I recently had a friend tell me that he doesn't do favors for people. I was surprised to hear him say this because his demeanor and actions seemed to say otherwise. Then he went on to clarify:

> I don't do favors because then there is an inherent sense of debt. And when there's a debt not repaid— or insufficiently repaid—there's disappointment. And when there's disappointment, there could be a breach

of trust in that relationship. So, I choose to be generous and give without the expectation of return, therefore eliminating the sense of a debt needing to be repaid.

As I pondered this, I realized his generosity was not only wise, but an *exercise in kindness*—one that protects relationships and puts love into action.

He's a smart man, and I'm grateful he's part of my inner circle!

What kindness looks like	What a lack of kindness looks like
Helping others without expectations of reciprocity	Keeping score and expecting a return
Speaking with words of love and respect	Harshness Sarcasm or avoidance
Practicing empathy	Being dismissive Indifference
Giving encouragement when needed	Tearing down Pride Indifference to helping someone when needed
A genuine perspective on helping others in need	A sense of superiority or ambivalence toward helping others

REFLECTION

Who has shown you true kindness recently,
and how can you pass it on this week?

Closing Thought

Kindness is not measured by the size of the gesture but by the sincerity of the heart behind it. Whether through a word, a gesture, or a listening ear, your kindness has the power to soften hearts and remind others that they are seen and valued. Choose to be kind as an act of love.

Virtue #5 – Forgiveness: Attempting to Restore Peace and Relational Harmony

Without forgiveness, relationships are damaged and fail to return to the richness they once had. Trust, which can act like glue in healthy relationships, is no longer present, and communication becomes strained or nonexistent.

Forgiveness does not mean denying that you were hurt, but rather acknowledging the offense and then making a conscious decision to release the anger and pain associated with it. Forgiveness of a former friend can free you from the burdens associated with anxiety, lack of trust, and stress—all harming your mental and physical health. Forgiveness allows both parties to move forward rather than remain stuck in unresolved conflicts. Forgiveness fosters trust, openness, and a renewed commitment to the relationship. Forgiveness, like the virtue of honesty, can strengthen a relationship. It's an investment!

> *Forgiveness does not mean denying that you were hurt.*

The need to be right opposes forgiveness. If you admit that anyone can make a mistake, it opens the thought process to consider your friend's perspective. Would you want to define your friend's character negatively after one event or misunderstanding? Would you want your own character defined that way? Having the ability to release resentment and bitterness through forgiveness not only has the potential to restore a relationship, but it also frees you from the pain.

As a pastor, I have heard an abundance of stories about individuals who have emotionally hurt people or been hurt. Not all of those stories included restoration through forgiveness; in fact, I would say the majority of those scenarios did not because of a lack of willingness to engage in honest conversation and a refusal to view the event with a different perspective.

I recall a conversation with a woman who suffered a significant emotional wound through an event with her husband. It had been years since their marriage had collapsed, and she struggled with moving forward. I asked her if they ever had a conversation about forgiveness. No! She was adamant that the conversation would not go anywhere, so I made a suggestion: "Write him a long letter—handwritten—explaining your hurt in detail, then extend forgiveness to free yourself from the bitterness that you harbor. But here's the catch: don't mail it to him, just read it in its entirety and then shred it." One or two weeks later, she was back in my office with an update from the exercise. She articulated that for the first time in years she felt free from the past. Was her letter a product of cheap grace? No, it was an exercise to express her pain without physical confrontation, which functioned as a vehicle for release. It worked for her, so maybe it could work for you! *Forgiveness does not and cannot change the past, but it can change the future!*

As we enter the fourth quarter of life, the virtue of forgiveness—the willingness both to extend it and to receive it—becomes invaluable, not only in marriage but in every relationship. Can your closest friend forgive? Do some of your friends or family members struggle with forgiveness? And if so, how should that shape your relationship with them? Only you can answer, but whatever the response, proceed with wisdom.

What forgiveness looks like	What a lack of forgiveness looks like
Releasing bitterness, resentment, and anger	Harboring a grudge or resentment
Extending grace when undeserved	Being adamant Unable to receive or extend grace
Acknowledgment of pain, but choosing not to live in it	Using your pain as leverage for manipulation
Choosing reconciliation	Avoidance

REFLECTION

Is there someone you need to forgive—not for their sake, but for your own peace and freedom? What would it take to release that burden?

Closing Thought

As stated earlier, forgiveness is not forgetting the past but refusing to be imprisoned by it. You deserve better! In your fourth quarter, the power of forgiveness lies in its ability to restore—not just relationships, but also your heart, your joy, and your legacy. Is someone waiting to hear your words of forgiveness so they can live free from the past? Are they waiting on you to accept their forgiveness?

Forgiveness is not forgetting the past but refusing to be imprisoned by it.

You can read more about forgiveness in chapter 6 titled "Spiritually Anchored."

Virtue #6 – Gratitude: A Conscious Choice of Focus

A friend of mine had more wealth than anyone I had ever met and was always filled with gratitude. It wasn't his wealth which made him grateful—it was his ability to give it away that stirred such deep appreciation in him.

If you had to choose between having gratitude or abundance—whether in the form of material goods, wealth, or general happiness—what would you choose and why? While both seem intricately linked, gratitude is *internal,* while abundance and happiness are derived from *external* influences.

Gratitude is a sense of appreciation cultivated through perspective. When appreciation becomes the lens through which one views life, it brings joy.

As a biblical precept, gratitude is clearly emphasized. Consider 1Thessalonians 5:16–18, Colossians 3:17, and Ephesians 5:20. These verses exemplify a perspective of thankfulness and appreciation. I encourage you to read them for a deeper insight.

A person filled with gratitude has learned to be content, finding joy and happiness without an abundance of external stimuli. This is not to say that abundance makes one thankless—many wealthy individuals show deep gratitude too. Choosing friends with the virtue of genuine gratitude is important because their joy is infectious and they are enjoyable to be around.

Having gratitude means you can acknowledge and appreciate the good in your relationships, and your friends or spouse will also value your contentment and appreciation in the connection.

What gratitude looks like	What a lack of gratitude looks like
Expressing appreciation	Complaining
Acknowledging others' kindness	Taking people or situations for granted
Being content with what you have	Never having enough or the right thing
Saying thank you with sincerity	Rarely saying thank you or expressing appreciation

REFLECTION

What is something, or someone, you may have taken
for granted who deserves your gratitude today?
Are you consistently looking for the positives in
your life and being content?

Closing Thought

Gratitude doesn't require everything to be perfect; it simply requires awareness. It's a conscious choice to focus on what you have, not what you lack. Let your life, especially in this fourth quarter, be marked by a spirit of gratitude. This virtue will become part of your legacy.

Virtue #7 – Perseverance: Staying the Course

When a couple marries before they have experienced trials and tribulations together, neither partner can say with certainty how the other will respond when difficulties arise. In essence, their relationship has not yet been tested. Marriages are meant to be deep, meaningful, and relationally rich. Perseverance in marriage is the ability to stay the course through hardship and to fulfill commitments, emerging stronger through experience. Without a commitment to persevere, it might be tempting for them to abandon their marriage in the face of adversity.

Loretta and Bill

When Loretta and Bill (names have been changed) were married, neither of them had a relationship with the Lord. Soon after their wedding, Loretta gave her life to Jesus, but Bill continually rejected the idea of faith. Throughout nearly fifty years of marriage, Bill quietly watched Loretta live her life as a believer. Occasionally, he would comment on how her decisions seemed to be influenced by her faith. He never challenged or criticized her—he simply observed.

Then, around their fiftieth wedding anniversary, Bill found himself on his deathbed in the hospital. With little energy and time remaining, he told Loretta that he had been watching and listening to her for fifty years and was ready to receive Jesus as his Lord. They prayed together and Bill put his faith in Jesus. Shortly after, Loretta became a widow, but with the peace of knowing that Bill had said yes to Jesus.

Loretta's life is an example of perseverance in its quietest, most faithful form—loving someone consistently over time. If you've ever supported a family member or friend through a long, difficult season—or had someone do the same for you—

your perseverance reflected love, loyalty, and an unwavering commitment when it was needed most.

Not all stories of perseverance involve marriage. Bonds and commitments to friends or to a cause can share these same enduring qualities. Whether standing beside someone through illness, adversity, or personal growth, perseverance is the trait that sees love and conviction through to the end.

What perseverance looks like	What a lack of perseverance looks like
Remaining consistent through trials	Giving up when things get tough
Supporting a person or a cause consistently	Little commitment, especially when faced with adversity
Staying true to promises	Breaking promises
Patience and endurance	Abandonment

REFLECTIVE QUESTION

Is there a relationship or commitment in your life that could benefit from renewed perseverance?

Closing Thought

Perseverance is not always grand or dramatic—it is often the quiet, steady resolve to love, support, and remain faithful over time. In relationships, this virtue builds trust and deepens bonds that withstand the trials of life. Stay the course, even when it feels challenging, knowing that your commitment speaks volumes about your love and character.

Virtue #8 – Empathy: Walking in Someone Else's Shoes

Empathy is "the action of understanding, being aware of, being sensitive to, and vicariously experiencing the feelings, thoughts, and experiences of another."[1]

Several years ago, I was preparing to officiate a funeral. In my preparation, I came across an article that described empathy and compassion in a profoundly moving way:

> Did you ever take a real trip down inside the broken heart of a friend? To feel the sob of the soul—the raw, red crucible of emotional agony? To have this become almost as much yours as that of your soul-crushed neighbor? Then, to sit down with him—and silently weep? This is the beginning of compassion.
>
> —Jess Moody[2]

While compassion involves taking action to help with a person's problem, empathy focuses on emotionally identifying with that person's experience. Empathy from a friend or family member might look like *sensing that something is wrong* before a word is even spoken. It may come through noticing subtle changes in behavior or mood, or simply sitting quietly with someone in their pain. Empathic people aren't quick to offer solutions—they first listen, connect, and feel.

---

[1] Merriam-Webster. "Empathy." Merriam-Webster.com Dictionary. https://www.merriam-webster.com/dictionary/empathy

[2] Jess Moody, "Quote-Unquote," SoundLiving.org, http://soundliving.org/compassion/

When we face difficult life events—death, relational struggles, or the loss of unfulfilled expectations—the best friend we can have is one who possesses the virtue of empathy. As the earlier quote so beautifully expresses, a person who patiently walks beside you, listens without judgment, and holds your heart with care is a rare and precious gift. These are the people you want in your inner circle.

If building friendships is like forming a team, in which each member holds similar values but offers unique strengths, a friend who exemplifies empathy will be among your most trusted confidants.

What empathy looks like	What a lack of empathy looks like
Listening intently without interruption	Dismissing or minimizing one's pain
Noticing emotional shifts and inquiring	Dismissing observations of noticeable difficulties
Expressing understanding with gentle words	Changing the subject or distancing through body language when the situation becomes uncomfortable
Validating one's experience	Making the experience about themselves, not the person in pain

REFLECTIVE QUESTION

When a friend or loved one shares something painful
with you, do you seek to understand their heart or
simply rush to solve the issue?

Closing Thought

Empathy doesn't require us to have all the answers. It invites us simply to *be present*. In a world quick to respond and slow to listen, the gift of empathy is a healing presence. Cultivating empathy in our relationships creates a sacred space where pain is honored, trust is built, and love is made visible.

> *Empathy doesn't require us to have all the*
> *answers. It invites us simply to be present.*

In my first book, *When It's Time© End-of-Life Planning at Any Age: Make it Part of Your Legacy*, I introduce a concept I call "The Ministry of Presence," in which your role is to sit beside the hurting person and listen, listen some more, and keep listening until they are tired of talking.."[3]

Virtue #9 – Generosity: Finding Joy in Giving Freely

Generosity is commonly equated with financial giving—such as charitable giving to religious organizations or other nonprofits, benevolent support during national or international disasters, and giving aid to those facing hunger or medical crises. These forms of giving, though essential, represent only one expression of generosity.

To deepen our understanding, we must also consider the generosity of time, presence, resources, and wisdom. This broader concept is explored more fully in chapter 4, "Vocationally Aligned." In truth, giving of one's time and sharing wisdom may be the most demanding expressions of generosity because

---

[3] Rick Craig, *When It's Time®, End-of-Life Planning at Any Age: Make it Part of Your Legacy* (Bella Matt Press), 184.

they require personal commitment. For many busy individuals, it's far easier to write a check or drop a few dollars into a box than to volunteer or give of their time.

While virtues are moral standards of what is good, right, and admirable, character traits describe tendencies or habits: being introverted or extroverted, honest, funny, accountable, resilient, or disciplined, as examples.

Surrounding yourself with generous people can help you grow in this area. Their example becomes an invitation. The biblical precept "It is more blessed to give than to receive" (Acts 20:35) isn't just a spiritual truth—it's a principle for building a meaningful life. Generosity impacts both the giver and the recipient by deepening connections, instilling gratitude, and shifting focus away from self and towards others.

What generosity looks like	What a lack of generosity looks like
Freely giving and responding to needs	Withholding money, time, and energy out of self-interest
Sharing resources without the expectation of return or recognition	Giving only when there is an anticipated gain
Volunteering consistently	Being only self-focused with spare time

REFLECTIVE THOUGHT

In your relationships, are you known as someone who gives freely or hesitantly? What small shift could you make this week to grow in generosity? What is the catalyst for your acts of generosity?

Closing Thought

True generosity flows not from abundance but from the heart. It's not about how much we give but how freely we give of ourselves: our time, our kindness, and our presence. A generous life is a joyful life, and one that reflects gratitude.

Virtue #10 – Courage: Moral Strength

Recklessness is acting impulsively without considering the consequences, while courage is grounded in conviction and born of wisdom, self-control, thoughtful consideration, and clarity, even in the face of fear. Courage means being willing to endure foreseeable consequences, even if success is uncertain. It is not the absence of fear, but the decision to act despite it.

When I think about courage, I reflect on my father's military service in the Royal Canadian Navy during World War II. At just seventeen, he was not honest about his age so that he could volunteer to join the Navy. After completing basic training, he served as a gunner aboard a Corvette-class vessel, patrolling the Atlantic Ocean and escorting naval ships from Nova Scotia and Newfoundland to England.

He didn't share much about his Navy career because of how deeply impacted he was by his experience on board his ship. Today, we recognize the courage it took to fulfill that mission. But courage often comes with a cost: My father, like others who served, struggled with what we now know as post-traumatic stress disorder (PTSD). Every person involved in military service, regardless of the era, embodies some degree of courage but may also carry unseen wounds.

Courage is not only found on the battlefield. Physical courage, though admirable and necessary, is only one kind. There is also moral courage—standing for what is right even when it's unpopular; spiritual courage—holding to one's faith in seasons of uncertainty; and emotional courage—choosing vulnerability, seeking healing, or forgiving when it's hard. As we journey through life, there will be times when we feel unequipped to respond with courage. In those moments, having friends who walk alongside us and who speak encouragement without pushing us toward recklessness is a true gift. These friends can mentor us through difficulty, helping us discover and live out a courage that is thoughtful, grounded, and strong.

What courage looks like	What a lack of courage looks like
Standing for what is right, even if you stand alone	Remaining silent when you can make a difference
Taking responsibility	Avoiding responsibility to protect oneself
Showing vulnerability and admitting weaknesses or failure	Showing comfort or protectionism over character
Defending the marginalized or mistreated	Standing by when in the face of wrongdoing

REFLECTIVE THOUGHT

When was the last time you chose to act courageously?
Were you motivated by conviction?
What did you learn about yourself?
Will courage be mentioned in your legacy?

Closing Thought

Whether standing alone in conviction or walking with someone through their trial, courage reminds us that our character is often defined in life's most difficult moments. Don't let fear rob you of the opportunity to display courage.

Virtue #11 – Self-Control: Enabling Trust and Respect Through Stability

You may have heard the fictional story of an experienced pilot flying a commercial aircraft. Mid-flight, the plane begins experiencing engine trouble. The pilot calmly announces over the intercom, "We're having issues with our number one engine, so we'll be shutting it down, but don't worry—we still have three fully functioning engines." Moments later, he returns: "We now need to shut down the number two engine due to similar issues. But two engines are more than enough to keep us airborne as we divert to the nearest airport." The passengers grow tense but remain hopeful. Then the pilot comes back over the intercom once more and announces that the number three engine has also failed. He concludes with, "We have only one engine remaining, but with a slow descent and just thirty minutes to our destination, I can maintain enough altitude to land us safely. This is your pilot—I'll see you after we land." That is self-control.

Self-control is the ability to regulate emotions, thoughts, and behaviors—to choose a measured response, or at times, no response at all. The wise person who practices self-control may live by the saying, "Better to be thought a fool than to open one's mouth and remove all doubt." Too many people miss golden opportunities to say absolutely nothing due to a lack of self-control.

In relationships, self-control nurtures emotional stability, cultivates safety, and builds trust. It gives us the ability to pause, reflect, and respond with intention rather than react in ways we may later regret. Most of us have felt the sting of sharp words, erratic behavior, or emotional volatility. When that happens, wisdom calls us to consider carefully how, and even if, we should remain in close connection.

When I sought counsel about this virtue, a wise friend stated it this way: "When in the company of someone who lacks self-control, there are moments when self-preservation must be paramount." I agree wholeheartedly. This virtue becomes non-negotiable when you audit the character of your closest relationships and the virtues you aspire to cultivate in your own life.

Reflecting back on the fictional story of the pilot, you may be thinking, *That pilot had a lot of training, so of course they had self-control.* But training isn't the only factor; self-control is something you can develop with practice and support. If you find yourself struggling in this area, don't hesitate to seek help. Your growth matters not only for you but also for your friends, your family, and all those who count on you.

What self-control looks like	What a lack of self-control looks like
Pausing before reacting, especially in highly emotional situations	Being quick to react, often emotionally or irrationally
Choosing words or timing carefully before responding	Allowing anger or frustration to control one's thoughts and actions
Managing impulses in all areas of life, such as spending, eating, and speech	Difficulty in managing impulses
Consistency of behavior in relationships	Volatile and inconsistent behavior

REFLECTIVE THOUGHT

Can you recall a time when your self-control
strengthened a relationship, or when a lack of it created
distance? What did you learn from this experience?

Closing Thought

Self-control may not get the same recognition as boldness or
passion, but it is the steady force that upholds trust, invites respect, and sustains healthy relationships. In choosing calm over
chaos, we show our true strength.

TAKING STOCK OF YOUR RELATIONSHIPS

"Your true belongings are not your possessions, but your relationships, the people to whom you belong and who belong to
you."[4] Dr. Alan Ahlgrim's statement is a refreshing contradiction
to what our culture and corporate America want us to believe.
We are indoctrinated to believe that material wealth equals success, prestige, and respect.

As a pastor, I have officiated more than 265 funeral and memorial services as I write this book. When I interview a family
to learn more about the deceased, I hear comments from survivors, such as "my dearest friend, who has incredible admin-
istrative skills, is helping me with the legal matters," or "I'm an
emotional mess, but my friend is helping me to calm down; she
just sits and listens to me," or "My brother was always the one

---

[4] Alan Ahlgrim, *Soul Strength: Rhythms for Thriving* (Colorado Springs, CO:
Illumify Media Global, 2022), 49.

who would help me with things like this," and "With my friend's help, together we are cleaning out his house. What would I do without my friend?"

If you were going through a difficult time, which of your friends would you count on to be there for you? If you have not already, think about each one of your closest friends and what they contribute to your friendship. Their contribution could show the strength of your friendship when it's most needed.

I have friends whom I shoot trap and skeet with, or practice at the pistol range with, that offer camaraderie and entertainment while providing insight and suggestions for improving my skills. With other friends, I sit and discuss deep spiritual matters because they have immersed themselves in their faith and speak with authority. I also have two friends I call upon for deep conversations and wisdom about personal struggles or when I'm at an impasse. Then there are friends from high school with whom I share past experiences or common interests.

Whether you have a wide circle of friends or prefer just a few close ones, I encourage you to take an honest look at each relationship and reflect on the role it plays in your life. Consider making a note about each one and placing it into a category such as acts of service, intellectual, spiritual, generous, fun, entertaining, mentoring, vocational, romantic, new friends, conscientious, or life-giving friends—or any other categories that fit your journey. This kind of reflection is important because time is precious, especially in fourth-quarter living.

If you notice life-giving relationships that deserve more deliberate attention, then I encourage you to invest in them. These friendships bring fulfillment and purpose to your life, and they also shape the legacy you are authoring each day—through the choices you make and the company you keep. I believe that your legacy can be the most enduring gift you leave for your family and friends.

Once you have created categories and a list of names and at-tributes under each one, review your findings to identify where your strengths and weaknesses show up in the context of cur-rent friendships. Make two columns—one for strengths and one for weaknesses. Doing this myself years ago, I learned two les-sons: First, I was quickly able to identify my life-giving friends and understand why I was drawn to their friendship. Secondly, I identified the relationships that required more time, energy, and the need for boundaries. These relationships were toxic or one-sided, leaving the relationship unbalanced and filling me with a feeling of obligation or guilt.

As you finalize your list and review it, you may find that there could be a need to expand the number of friends you have in the Strength column. Dr. Alan Ahlgrim raises this question: "Choosing Quality Over Quantity. How many quality relation-ships do you enjoy? Sadly, we live in an age of amazing tech-nological connection yet soul-depleting personal disconnection. While many have hundreds of Facebook friends, most have few face-to-face, personal friends."[5] I agree—I hear it regularly while in general conversations and talking with survivors. But there's good news to embrace: This can change when you live with pur-pose in mind.

Taking your list and reviewing both columns—Strength and Weakness—identify your strengths and celebrate them with gratitude. As you review your column titled Weakness, identify people with the attributes that compel you to foster a deeper connection. Over the years, I have found that I am blessed to have such a variety of friends, but it took investing time and en-ergy. Give as much time to these relationships as you expect to receive; these are reciprocal relationships that are balanced and life-giving, especially in fourth-quarter living.

---

[5] Ahlgrim, *Soul Strength,* 53

To draw a comparison of relationships developed when we were younger versus living in the fourth quarter, think of the bond developed between military and first responder personnel in their second and third quarters. Their experiences are life-changing, and the bond through those experiences will not be forgotten. But unless those relationships continue through investment, they remain as memories, not active relationships that are reciprocal. There is a vast difference between old friendships and those you choose to keep active.

RECOGNIZING YOUR INNER CIRCLE

The previous exercise under "Taking Stock of Your Relationships" was designed to help you identify your *inner circle* of friends. These friends are the ones who encourage you, know your challenges, and keep that information confidential. Your relationship is reciprocal, meaning both you and they mutually contribute to the health of the relationship as a show of respect and appreciation.

Your inner circle of friends and family should have the ability to counsel, motivate, challenge, encourage, offer companionship, be emotionally healthy, and have a history of facing trials and tribulations wisely. Putting this circle together is not as difficult as it appears, and since you have already performed an audit on your current friends and have identified each relationship's strengths and weaknesses, your plan has already begun.

When you consider this small group of friends as the inner circle, where does that leave other relationships? One concept to adopt is the concentric ring model, as shown below.

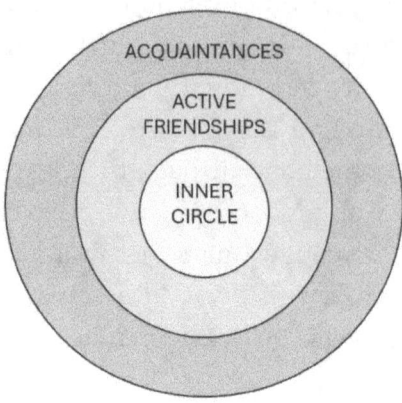

The Concentric Ring Model

An inner circle of friends might only consist of 3–6 people: those you have the strongest connection with, as discussed above. These are the ones who fit the description I offered in the previous paragraph. Moving outward is another group of friends we'll call *active friendships.*

Active friendships normally live in your area. You see them regularly through events, church, or the workplace. They may be parents of your children's friends, but they do not possess the same history of investment and attributes as those of your inner circle. They could become part of your inner circle in the future since you already have a form of regular contact, provided they possess the attributes you admire and aspire to.

Acquaintances belong in the outer ring of the circle of friends. With minimal investment in these relationships, they are people you see only on occasion. They often remain in this ring not out of disregard but because of limited time, differing priorities, or past experiences.

I'm reminded of a proverb found in the Hebrew Scriptures (Old Testament) that offers a visual of what your inner circle may consist of. Proverbs 18:24 says, "A man of many companions may come to ruin, but there is a friend who sticks closer than a brother" (ESV). What this proverb is saying echoes this chapter on being relationally rich: Blessed with a few strong and enduring relationships is far superior to having a multitude of friends who offer no support.

LIVING LIFE IN COMMUNITY

There was a time in our culture when you would hear the word "community," or "living in a community," which referenced your home address and your surrounding neighbors and businesses. My first real sense of living in a community was in the early '60s, when our family lived in an apartment in Anaheim, California, as I mentioned earlier.

Our apartment complex was the length of a city block, and there were at least thirty kids my age close by. It was great! We shared our street name, similar family dynamics, local schools, common interests, such as playing sports, watching the Disneyland fireworks from our street corner, and running home to meet our curfew. All these shared moments made us a community.

Another lifestyle in the '60s included the iconic "live free, anti-establishment generation" that ushered in terms like "communes," "colonies," and "encampments." Today, residential and commercial communities are designated with poetic names. Even local coffee shops use the term "community" as a marketing attempt to make patrons feel at home with other like-minded people, projecting an active, safe, and friendly atmosphere. Some websites market to a named collection of like-minded people, giving them a perceived sense of support and understanding within their group. Our culture has transitioned from tangible communities to organizing meetups at designated areas like sports fields, community centers, schools, churches, or playgrounds for kids. But what about communities for people who are living in their fourth quarter?

Living life in a community of friends and family is one of the hallmarks of fourth-quarter living, and this community needs to have space for deeper relationships, offering more than casually meeting someone for coffee or sharing the community's name. As I outlined above, in "Recognizing Your Inner Circle," strong relationships tend to have a deeper sense of value and purpose.

A senior group at our church shared with me about their lifestyles and needs. One person told me a story of how several people would share the contents of a food item purchased at a big box store. Their reasoning made sense: Purchase a large container and then divide it to lower the cost. Not only did they shop and share, but they also checked in nightly with their assigned person to ensure they were safe and healthy. They even shared rides almost everywhere they went. More than all of their cost-saving techniques combined, they were doing life together, and it brought them joy, camaraderie, and a sense of purpose.

Here's what I learned from my friends:

1. **Support and Encouragement:** Life isn't getting easier as we age; it is becoming more difficult. But through creative thinking and application, they were meeting each other's needs and loved being together. They are a community of people with common interests and needs, and they support and celebrate their victories together.

2. **Wisdom Shared:** A good community shares ideas that translate into life lessons. All generations should learn the wisdom these wonderful people have gained over their life journeys.

3. **Living Life with Purpose:** The fourth quarter of life includes accountability to stay focused, motivated, engaged, active, and growing. Too often, we hear that loneliness is commonplace. Living life with purpose in the fourth quarter is designed to combat this while offering a sense of fulfillment and hope.

4. **Emotional and Spiritual Fulfillment:** Whether you are a person of faith or not, it's difficult to argue against the fact that humans are created to be relational. Through relationships, you find common interests and bonds. When you find a friend you can place in your inner circle—one with the virtue(s) to walk with you during emotional times—you are living out the true sense of community. You actively sought virtues in others and forged new friendships, and now you get to benefit from those relationships by being known, supported, and loved.

If you have not already, I strongly encourage you to take the time to invest in becoming relationally rich in your fourth quarter. It will be well worth it!

CHAPTER 3

PHYSICALLY FIT

By Bill Nesbitt, MD,
and Lynne Nachtrieb, RDN, CSO

Being physically fit is not a one-size-fits-all term. Age, genetic predisposition, and lifestyle choices are all components of how we age physically. As we enter our fourth quarter, our definition of what physically fit means will change, while the need for fitness increases.

I have called upon my friend, Dr. Nesbitt, who specializes in hospice care, to share his experiences from decades of practice. Dr. Nesbitt tells his story as an allegory because it softens the anticipated medical jargon. As we collaborated, there was agreement that the reader should not take any part of his story verbatim and apply it to themselves, but rather, learn from his experiences and contact their physician for personal care.

I am convinced that once you begin reading his story, you will be drawn into the genre—like attending a play or watching a movie. Dr. Nesbitt has meticulously built personalities into his patients (fictitious characters), adding surprises to anticipated outcomes. It is my privilege to introduce Dr. Nesbitt. (I will introduce Lynne afterward.)

The vast majority of medical issues that impact the quality and length of our lives occur in the final quarter of our earthly existence. As life expectancy in the US approaches seventy-eight years—the average age for men and women combined—we had better be aware of, and prepared for, the myriad of problems that can occur in old age, and the measures that can be taken to avoid or mitigate them early on.

This chapter will address a few of the most common issues that our geriatric population faces. However, it is important to understand that every individual is unique, and all medical care needs to be custom-tailored to the specific patient by a well-trained, conscientious, and compassionate physician—one who takes into account every facet of the patient's health, life, and social context. [Note: This chapter must not be considered medical advice for any specific person, save for the fictional characters in the story below.]

A few general guidelines will be addressed, ones that can make all the difference in how to flourish in what can be the best years of your life. We will address five general areas of geriatric care: preventive measures, chronic illness, terminal illness, caregiver survival tips, and fascinating new research that appears to show that our consciousness (spirit) survives the death of our body. Come with me as we follow Jim and Jane Smith, a fictional couple, seeking their medical care from a fictional country doc in a rural practice much like mine.

Jim and Jane Smith

The crisp morning air brings the excitement of change. As I drive along the winding country road toward my clinic in the Sierra foothills, I smell the first scent of burning leaves and pine needles heralding the coming of the last season of another year. The cooler weather also triggers the arthritis in my right knee, a reminder that I am also entering the final season of my life. I think back over the years, reviewing how I became who I am today.

I recall many long hours helping my patients, many personal triumphs and failures, the lessons and rewards of marriage and raising a family, and the incredible blessings of grandchildren. I reflect on how it was both the blessings and tragedies, the prudent choices as well as my mistakes, that have forged my life and rewarded me with painfully earned wisdom.

This journey has resulted in feeling profoundly thankful and rich in relationships and in the love of family and friends. I thank God that my work not only allows me to help heal the bodies of my patients but also gives me the opportunity to help them steer their lives to avoid the pitfalls I encountered on my way, and assist them in finding the meaning and richness that a well-lived life can bring.

My small clinic sits at the edge of our tiny town nestled in the hills, where the proud valley oaks finally give way to the majestic pines of the towering mountains. My first patients of the morning are Jim and Jane Smith, here for their annual exams. I pause at my desk to review their charts before heading to the exam room. I've been their doctor for more than twenty years now. Like many of my patients in their early sixties, they're also navigating their fourth quarter of life—that crucial period when maintaining health requires both wisdom and vigilance.

"Hey, lovebirds, how ya doin'?" I greet them as I enter. "How are the kids? Are they getting any sleep with the new grandbaby? I don't suppose you have any photos of the little critter?"

Smiles break out, as do cell phones. After some brief oohing and ahhing over pictures of their newest grandchild, we get down to business.

This visit is for their annual Medicare wellness exams, and it provides a perfect opportunity to review the "seven pillars" of fourth-quarter geriatric health. Jim and Jane filled out the health questionnaire before the appointment. These questions gather information and address recommendations such as:

1. **Preventive care** – regular health screenings; appropriate vaccinations; dental, visual, and hearing evaluations; medication reviews; and early detection of diseases and corresponding intervention strategies

2. **System-by-system monitoring** – to monitor the health of major body systems

   — Cardiovascular: blood pressure, heart rhythm, circulation, exercise tolerance, and medication effectiveness
   — Respiratory: Breathing patterns, exercise capacity, infection prevention, sleep quality, and energy levels
   — Digestive: Nutrition, bowel habits, appetite, weight maintenance, and hydration

3. **Functional assessment** – evaluates physical ability through mobility and balance testing, strength and flexibility checks, and coordination and physical independence tests

4. **Cognitive health** – assesses mental functioning: memory, problem-solving, language and communication, attention span, and executive function

5. **Social engagement** – reviews connections and mental stimulation through family connections, community involvement, participation in activities, support systems and other opportunities for engagement

6. **Safety and independence** – ensures a secure and supportive living situation by assessing home safety and fall risk, medication management, emergency preparedness, and use of adaptive equipment

7. **Quality of life** – addresses overall well-being, including pain management, sleep quality, emotional health, and personal goals and life satisfaction

We discuss normal patterns of aging: gradual decrease in height (half an inch per decade after forty), slightly slower movement and reaction time, mild morning stiffness lasting under thirty minutes, reduced flexibility and strength, changed sleep patterns (lighter sleep, earlier waking), a decreased thirst sensation, slower digestion, mild changes in memory and word finding, some reduction in taste and smell, and adapted balance responses.

I highlight things requiring medical attention, which include sudden height loss of more than half an inch, significant balance problems or unexplained falls, severe joint pain or prolonged morning stiffness, excessive daytime sleepiness, rapid decline in strength or stamina, new onset shortness of breath, unexplained weight loss (10 pounds or more), new pain patterns, significant sensory changes, persistent digestive changes, and notable memory lapses.

Jane gives me her blood pressure log. Her blood pressure readings open an important discussion about cardiovascular health. "It's reading 148 over 88 today," I note, "a bit higher than I'd like to see. Let's talk about how your heart health routine has been going." This launches us into a deeper conversation about the changes that come with aging, and how to distinguish normal shifts from warning signs that need attention.

Jane's cardiovascular risks include hypertension, hyperlipidemia, and diabetes, so we review the checklist of comprehensive cardiovascular care:

Daily Monitoring. Blood Pressure and Blood Sugar Management:

- Morning readings before medications or eating
- Evening checks if prescribed
- Record-keeping system
- Position-changes awareness
- Salt and sugar intake tracking
- Heart and Diabetes Health Markers:
- Pulse regularity
- Exercise tolerance
- Breathing patterns
- Swelling checks
- Weight stability

Lifestyle Modifications. Exercise Program:

- Morning walks starting at 10 minutes
- Seated exercises during TV time
- Standing exercises at the kitchen counter
- Stair climbing when able
- Regular stretching
- Balance activities

Dietary Approaches:

- Reduced sodium without sacrificing taste
- Increased potassium-rich foods
- Mediterranean diet principles
- Proper hydration schedule
- Portion control strategies
- Meal-timing optimization

Medication Management. Organization:

- Weekly pill organizers
- Medication schedule chart
- Side effect monitoring
- Interaction awareness
- Regular medication reviews
- Emergency supply maintenance

Diabetes management:

- **Eat healthy**: Choose what, when, and how much to eat. Carbohydrates affect blood sugar more than other nutrients, so follow a meal plan to regulate how much to eat.
- **Exercise**: Aim for at least 2.5 hours of moderate to vigorous exercise per week, and try to do muscle-strengthening exercises at least twice a week.
- **Take medication**: Take your medications as prescribed, even if you feel good. If you think you're having a problem with your medicine, call your doctor or the nurse's advice line.
- **Monitor blood sugar**: Test your blood sugar often, and keep a logbook to track your A1C (average blood sugar), blood pressure, and cholesterol.
- **Manage stress**: Learn ways to manage stress and cope with the emotional side of diabetes.
- **Get checkups**: Go to checkups and get tested for kidney disease annually.
- **Limit alcohol**: If you drink alcohol, get your healthcare professional's okay first. Choose light beer and dry wines, or use sugar-free mixers. Eat before drinking or drink with a meal to prevent low blood sugar. Check your blood sugar before bed.

Jane mentions trouble sleeping lately and difficulty keeping up with her garden. "The spirit's willing," she says with a rueful smile, "but the body sometimes argues back." This leads us into a detailed discussion of energy conservation and activity modification. I explain how managing energy throughout the day is budgeting, the same as you would do with your monthly income. You need to prioritize your resources and use them wisely.

"You know," I tell them both, "as I mentioned, the changes with aging can be natural and gradual, while other changes might signal something that needs urgent attention." I explain how normal aging brings gradual changes, but how there can be changes that warrant closer attention, such as sudden dizziness, unexplained weight loss, new patterns of pain, or significant changes in memory or thinking.

"First, let's talk about movement," I begin. "Walking is still the best medicine we have. Start with ten minutes after each meal—it helps digestion and your heart. When you're watching TV, try doing simple exercises during commercials. Even standing up and sitting down a few times builds strength."

I show Jane how to take accurate blood pressure readings at home, explaining the importance of timing. "Check it before medications in the morning and again in the evening. Keep a log; patterns tell us more than single readings."

We discuss dietary changes that don't feel like punishment. "Instead of saying 'no salt,' let's talk about flavoring food differently. Fresh herbs from your garden, a squeeze of lemon, roasted garlic—these can make food tasty without raising blood pressure."

She writes everything down in a small notebook—something I've always appreciated about Jane. "What about my morning stiffness, Doc? Some days it's harder to get going."

This leads us naturally into discussing joint health and flexibility. I explain how our joints are mostly mechanical things; they need regular movement and use to stay functional. Some morning stiffness is natural, but severe or prolonged stiffness needs attention.

"The key is to keep moving," I tell her. "Think of your joints like bearings in machinery—they need regular use to stay lubricated. Start each morning with gentle stretches before you even get out of bed. Point and flex your feet, rotate your ankles, bend and straighten your knees, make circles with your arms."

As I demonstrate these movements, I notice Jim watching intently. His own discomfort becomes more apparent as he shifts position again. When I check Jane's joints for range of motion, I explain how arthritis is a natural part of aging, but that there are many ways to manage it effectively. "Here are some ways to manage degenerative arthritis at home: Regular exercise can help keep joints flexible and strengthen muscles. Try low-impact activities like swimming, water aerobics, or weight training. Losing weight can reduce stress on joints and improve mobility.

"Applying heat or cold to affected joints can help relieve pain and stiffness. Heat increases blood flow and flexibility, while cold numbs nerves and reduces inflammation. You can use canes, walkers, shoe inserts, or braces to support joints and improve mobility. A mostly plant-based diet can reduce inflammation and pain. Food choices can even help. The best things to eat include fatty fish, olive oil, berries, garlic, ginger, broccoli, walnuts, spinach, and grapes. Foods to avoid include added sugars, processed meats, gluten, and foods high in salt.

"Try to avoid frequent bending or other repetitive motions. Balance activity with rest and don't overdo it. Remove hazards like throw rugs. Secure carpets and install slip mats on stairs. You can also add a stair lift or ramp and install guardrails on outdoor steps. Try acupuncture, massage, meditation, tai chi, or dietary supplements. Join a support group online or in your community to cope with the disease and learn how to manage symptoms."

I again notice Jim squirming in his chair, a grimace of pain on his face. I ask Jane if she would mind if I shifted my attention to Jim for a moment. "Oh yes," she says, "he really needs to talk to you about his back."

"Doc," Jim finally interjects, "speaking of stiffness and such …" He pauses, clearly uncomfortable with more than just his joints. "I've been having some other issues I need to discuss."

I recognize that hesitation. I've learned to read the subtle signs that tell me when a patient, particularly a male patient, is working up the courage to discuss sensitive health concerns. "Doc, I've had difficulty starting to urinate, and occasionally I see a little blood in my urine. At night, I've been having to get up four to five times to pee for months now. I've lost about fifteen pounds in the past three months without trying to diet. And for the past four to five months, I've developed a nagging pain in my back. I think it might be a bladder infection."

I have Jim give me a urine sample, which tests negative for infection. "Let's do your exam now, Jim," I say, giving him the opening he needs. As he moves to the examination table, his careful movements tell their own story. Beyond the obvious joint stiffness, I notice his moderate weight loss since his last visit—by the new notches he punched in his old leather belt. There is also a certain pallor to his complexion that concerns me. On examination of his prostate, I feel a large, hard mass in the left lobe.

I explain that we need further testing to rule out prostate cancer. Careful to balance honesty with hope, I tell him that every man will get it if he lives long enough, but the younger you are when it comes on, the more of a problem it can be. "These symptoms could have several causes," I tell him, "but we need to know exactly what we're dealing with." I outline the tests we'll run, including prostate-specific antigen (PSA) levels, X-rays of his back and pelvis, and other diagnostics that will give us a clearer picture.

On his follow-up visit, both Jim and Jane appear apprehensive. Jane reaches for Jim's hand as I prepare to discuss the test results. I tell him, "I'd like to take some time to discuss what's going on, so let's take a look at these results. The PSA results do suggest prostate cancer, but we won't know how serious it is without further testing. I'm going to refer you to a urologist for a biopsy. That way, we'll know just what we are dealing with and what we need to do for the best outcome."

On his return visit two weeks later, I tell Jim that the test results confirm my concerns about his prostate cancer, and the bone scan shows it has spread to the bones in his back and pelvis. Its aggressive nature demands immediate attention. "Give it to me straight, Doc," Jim says, his grip on Jane's hand tightening. "No sugarcoating."

Delivering difficult news never gets easier, but honesty delivered with compassion serves patients best. We discuss treatment options, and I let him know that the prognosis depends on how he responds to treatment. I explain how prostate cancer in older men can behave differently from that in younger patients, and why some treatments might be more appropriate than others.

"Let's make a plan," I say, spreading out information sheets on my desk. We discuss specialists, treatment protocols, and how to maintain quality of life throughout the process. Jim, ever practical, takes notes in his own small pocket notebook.

As we develop the treatment strategy, I keep a close eye on Jane. Caregivers often neglect their own health while focusing on their loved ones. Her blood pressure needs monitoring, her diabetes requires attention, and I know the stress of caregiving can exacerbate both conditions. "Remember," I tell them both, "this is a team effort. You've got me, your specialists, your family, and our whole clinic of staff behind you."

The next few months bring a steady rhythm of appointments, treatments, and adjustments. Jim faces each challenge with quiet determination, but I notice the toll it takes. Some days, he sits more heavily in the exam room chair, his bird-watching stories grow shorter, his jokes less frequent.

Over the next three months, Jim's disease is advancing despite all the interventions. The treatments, lab visits, scans, and specialist visits are sapping what little time and energy he has. "Doc, I don't want to do this anymore. Nothing's helping, and the chemo is just making me feel worse."

"Jim," I say, "I agree with you completely. Regardless of what we do, if the disease runs its usual course, you won't make it another six months. I think it's time we focused on your comfort and getting the most out of the time you have left." I introduce the concept of hospice. I tell him that it is not giving up, but rather accepting reality and making the most of his time left.

I explain to him that by converting his Medicare coverage to hospice, he will have all of his hospice-related medications covered, and the support of a hospice team—including a physician, case manager, registered nurse (RN), home health aide, social worker, chaplain, and volunteers.

His hospice care level can be modified from the standard home visits (at least every two weeks, more often as needed) to continuous 24-hour care, which is covered for crises requiring close monitoring by a nurse. If symptoms become too complex to manage at home, inpatient care can be provided for crisis situations. Additionally, if the primary caregiver is temporarily unable to provide care—such as during a family emergency or a personal health issue—up to a five-day respite stay is covered in a skilled nursing facility. Hospice care can be revoked by the patient or family at any time, and coverage reverts to Medicare as before. If the patient improves, the hospice may discharge the patient and readmit them when the condition declines again.

During each visit, I monitor Jim's physical changes while helping them both navigate the progression of his illness. During one appointment, while discussing his increasing fatigue, he shares an important insight.

"You know what I've learned, Doc? Watching those birds at my feeder teaches me something. They don't worry about tomorrow's seeds—they just fully live right now." His observation resonates with my decades of watching patients face terminal illness. Those who find peace often discover it in such simple moments of presence.

We adjust medications and strategies as symptoms change. When his pain increases, we discuss both pharmaceutical and nonpharmaceutical approaches. When his appetite decreases, we talk about small, nutrient-dense meals and protein supplements. Each symptom becomes a puzzle we solve together.

Jane's role as caregiver grows more demanding as Jim declines. While attending one of Jim's visits, I notice signs of strain in Jane—slight trembling in her hands as she takes notes, dark circles under her eyes, a moment of tearfulness when discussing Jim's treatment plan. This prompts our discussion about caregiver health maintenance.

"Remember," I tell her, "you can't pour from an empty pitcher. If you are going to take care of him, you have to take care of yourself first." I point out that a caregiving spouse needs increasing support, care, and surveillance as the needs of the ill spouse increase. I show her the lengthy list of things she needs to monitor, and she agrees to review it in detail and apply it to her situation.

COMPREHENSIVE CAREGIVER SUPPORT STRATEGY

1. Physical Health Maintenance

Daily Health Practices:

- Blood pressure monitoring
- Medication compliance
- Sleep hygiene
- Exercise routine
- Nutrition focus
- Stress reduction
- Regular breaks

Preventive Care:

- Medical appointments
- Health screenings
- Dental checkups
- Vision tests
- Vaccination updates
- Laboratory monitoring
- Bone density scans

2. Mental Health Support

Emotional Care:

- Stress management techniques
- Anxiety reduction strategies
- Depression screening
- Grief counseling
- Support group participation
- Individual therapy
- Spiritual support if desired

Social Connection:

- Family involvement
- Friend maintenance
- Community engagement
- Church participation
- Support group attendance
- Social activities
- Regular communication

3. Practical Support Implementation

Daily Management:

- Helper schedule creation
- Task delegation
- Meal preparation plans
- Housekeeping assistance
- Transportation arrangement
- Shopping support
- Medication management

Emergency Planning:

- Backup caregiver identification
- Emergency contact list
- Medical information organization
- Hospital bag preparation
- Home safety assessment
- Communication plan
- Resource list compilation

"What should we watch for when the end is getting near?" Jane asks during one visit. I explain the signs of approaching death: changes in breathing patterns, decreased interest in food and drink, withdrawal from conversation, and cool extremities. "But also watch for moments of clarity," I add. "Sometimes there are precious windows of connection near the end."

Within just a few short weeks, Jim peacefully and comfortably transitions to a new plane of existence. Jane is amazed at the great job the hospice did at keeping Jim's symptoms under control. Their support of Jane through this difficult ordeal made the grief bearable.

Several months after Jim's passing, Jane brings me a journal during her checkup. "I've been writing down things we learned through all this," she says, her hands steady on the worn notebook. "Thought it might help others facing this journey."

Through tear-filled eyes, she shares insights they gained: the importance of early symptom recognition, the value of maintaining dignity through adaptation rather than resignation, the crucial role of family support, and the unexpected gifts found in life's final season.

Their experience taught them practical lessons about navigating serious illness: how to modify daily activities without abandoning them entirely, ways to maintain independence through strategic adaptation, the importance of keeping social connections even when health declines, and the value of accepting help without losing autonomy.

Jane wistfully looks out the window at the gray skies and bare branches of winter. "You know, Doc, I really believe I will see him again. My faith tells me I will. Right before Jim took his final breath, he was actually talking to his mother. Wouldn't it be great if that were true?"

Jane continues her own health journey now, armed with deeper wisdom about aging, illness, and the end of life. She's become a resource for others in our community facing similar challenges. Her blood pressure has stabilized, her diabetes is better controlled, and she's found a new purpose in supporting others through their fourth-quarter challenges.

———

Through our years of medical practice, certain essential wisdom emerges about making the most of life's fourth quarter. These insights, gleaned from patients like Jim and Jane, might help others navigate this season.

Early recognition of health changes makes a crucial difference. Just as Jim's delayed reporting of symptoms impacted his options, prompt attention to changing health patterns often leads to better outcomes. Know your baseline health status and report significant changes promptly.

Maintain preventive care even when a serious illness is affecting a loved one. Jane's attention to her own health screenings and chronic conditions while caring for Jim allowed her to continue providing optimal support. Regular checkups, dental care, vision tests, and recommended screenings remain vital.

Modify activities rather than abandoning them. When Jim couldn't manage full woodworking sessions, he adapted by inviting a few of the young guys in his church to build ornate birdhouses, while he watched from a comfortable old chair a neighbor had put in his shop. When Jane's arthritis made gardening difficult, she switched to raised beds and adaptive tools. The goal isn't to stop living—it's to find new ways to do what matters.

Build support systems before they're critically needed. Establish relationships with healthcare providers, connect with community services, and strengthen family bonds. These networks provide crucial support during health challenges.

Remember that every season has its purpose. As Jim demonstrated through his birdwatching, sometimes slowing down allows us to notice life's subtle gifts. Even in the midst of illness, opportunities exist for learning, teaching, and finding meaning.

For those navigating their fourth quarter of life, whether as patients or caregivers, certain practical guidelines prove invaluable:

Managing Medications

Keep an updated list of all medications, including over-the-counter drugs and supplements.

Use pill organizers, set alarms for medication times, and regularly review medications with your doctor to ensure they're still necessary and effective.

Home Safety

Evaluate your home environment through the lens of mobility changes. Install handrails, improve lighting, secure rugs, and arrange furniture to allow clear pathways.

Consider bathroom modifications early, such as grab bars and a walk-in tub or shower modifications, before they become urgent needs.

Nutrition and Hydration

Maintain good nutrition even when your appetite decreases. Small, frequent meals often work better than three large ones.

Keep nutritious snacks easily accessible.

Remember that thirst sensation often decreases with age—make hydration a scheduled routine rather than relying on thirst.

Exercise and Movement

Stay active within your abilities. Even chair exercises contribute to strength and flexibility. Focus on activities that maintain balance, build strength, and promote heart health. Remember that some movement is always better than none.

Sleep Quality	Social Connections
Establish consistent sleep routines.	Maintain relationships with family and friends even when health challenges make it difficult.
Address factors that interrupt sleep, such as lighting, temperature, bathroom needs, and medication timing.	Use technology to stay connected when physical visits aren't possible.
Consider how naps affect nighttime sleep.	Accept invitations when able and be honest with friends about your energy limitations.
	Remember, patients on their deathbeds do not call for their bank statements, trophies, or awards. They call for those they love, the family and friends with whom they shared their lives.

As Jane's healing continues in the years following Jim's passing, she often shares additional insights during her visits. Her own journey through widowhood and aging brings a valuable perspective about life's fourth quarter. "What I've learned," she tells me during a recent checkup, "is that aging well is about adaptation, not surrender. Jim showed me that. Even in his final weeks, he found ways to contribute, to connect, to matter."

THE WISDOM OF FOURTH-QUARTER LIVING EMERGES THROUGH SUCH EXPERIENCES.

Maintain purpose. Whether through teaching others, sharing wisdom, or simply being present for loved ones, having purpose enriches life regardless of physical limitations.

Practice acceptance without resignation. Accept help when needed, but maintain independence where possible. Use adaptive devices not as symbols of decline, but as tools for continued engagement in life.

Share your story. Your experiences, both challenges and triumphs, can guide others. Jim and Jane's journey continues to help other patients navigate similar paths.

Plan ahead but live now. While advance planning matters, don't let preparation for tomorrow steal today's joy. As Jim discovered with his birds, each day brings its own gifts.

Most importantly, remember that the most important things in life are not things; they are relationships. The way to experience love is to show love to others. If you want friends, be a friend. Stop worrying; it does no good. Ninety percent of the things we fear will never occur. You can't change the past, so don't be chained to it. The future will likely be very different from what you fear, so take care of what you can change right now and leave the rest in God's hands.

Wealth is not how much you have, but how little you lack. Generous people always seem to be satisfied with what they have. Read the Sermon on the Mount (Matthew 5–7). It is important advice on how to live, given by the most important person ever born, Jesus, in the most important book in all of human history—the Bible.

Wealth is not how much you have,
but how little you lack.

For physicians like me, guiding patients through their fourth quarter requires both medical knowledge and deep humanity. We must understand not just the physiology of aging, but also its emotional, social, and spiritual dimensions.

Your fourth quarter can indeed be rich with meaning, connection, and purpose. While health challenges may arise, they need not define this season of life. Through proper medical care, proactive health management, strong support systems, and maintained engagement in life, these years can bring their own unique satisfaction.

Remember what Jim taught us through his journey: Every season has its gifts. Make them count.

―――

Lynne Nachtrieb RDN, CSO
(Registered Dietitian Nutritionist,
Certified Specialist in Oncology)

LIVING HEALTHY IN THE FOURTH QUARTER

Beyond the emotions and reflections, this chapter also seeks to offer tangible tools in the form of practical wisdom for everyday living. I believe that one of the keys to finishing strong in the fourth quarter of life is learning to adapt—intentionally and wisely—to the changing dynamics of our bodies. This includes understanding how food, medication, exercise, mental stimulation, and even environmental factors influence our well-being. While there is a plethora of factors contributing to a healthy life, these tend to be among the most significant and practical to address, from my experience.

With that in mind, I reached out to my friend and trusted colleague, Lynne Nachtrieb, a registered dietitian nutritionist with a deep well of experience and insight. For more than two decades, Lynne worked as a registered dietitian in the oncology department of a respected hospital, counseling individuals facing some of life's most difficult health challenges. She is deeply trusted, highly professional, and beloved by her patients, colleagues, and friends. Her wisdom is hard-earned and deeply human, and that is why her guidance is featured in this chapter.

To make the information provided both informative and engaging, Lynne will first respond to health topics with factual clarity. Then, in a unique literary twist, she'll take on the role of a fictional health columnist responding to letters from readers— fictional characters—based on real-life scenarios. These "Dear Lynne" letters add color and relatability to the conversation, offering wisdom in a more personal, storytelling format.

I trust you'll find Lynne's input both enlightening and enjoyable. Her voice brings not only scientific credibility but also compassion and practical application—exactly what we need to live well and finish strong.

————

As a registered dietitian working with various conditions and disease states, I have learned that the majority of us have developed eating habits requiring change to improve our nutritional status, especially as we live through our fourth quarter of life. Additionally, ongoing research in nutrition has revealed important findings that can impact our overall health, such as the important role of adequate fiber intake, the role of the gut microbiome, the body's inflammatory response, and how these relate to chronic illness. Studies have also highlighted the benefits of antioxidants, and phytonutrients (plant-based compounds), as well as the impact of certain foods and beverages on cancer risk.

There's another important aspect to living well in the fourth quarter of life: enjoying food and sharing it with those we care about most. We can do that with discipline and the desire to optimize our health through knowledge. Collectively, we share strong similarities, but each of us is different; therefore, understanding those differences empowers us to make better choices and live better.

A HEALTHY GUT

Every human has a particular blend of microbes—viruses, bacteria, and fungi—in their gut. This microbiome is shaped primarily by diet, environment, genetics, medications, and lifestyle. In fact, we have more microbes in our bodies than body cells. A more diverse gut microbiome is linked to better health. Eating a wide variety of fruits, vegetables, fiber-rich foods, whole grains, and fermented foods with probiotics—such as kefir, kombucha, yogurt, sauerkraut, or miso—supports this diversity. These microbes help digest fiber and nutrients, help control the immune system, and contribute to heart health. In contrast, processed foods, convenience foods, and too much sugar reduce bacterial diversity and negatively affect health.

As we age, the negative effects of proinflammatory foods present themselves and can contribute to chronic pain. These include added sugars, excessive omega-6 oils (safflower, sunflower, corn oils), high salt intake, red meat and processed meat, highly processed snack foods, refined carbohydrates (like white bread, pasta, rice), and too much alcohol.

The American Heart Association recommends a limit of 25 grams (6 teaspoons) of added sugars per day for women and 36 grams (9 teaspoons) for men. Food labels must now indicate how much added sugar a product contains. Whole foods, such as milk or fruit, only contain natural sugars, not added ones.

On the flip side, anti-inflammatory foods and nutrients can support health and optimize nutritional status. These include olive oil, avocado, fatty fish, nuts, seeds, olives, citrus fruits, vegetables, lentils, beans, herbs, spices, garlic, onion, and ginger. These foods are also rich in antioxidants and phytochemicals that help prevent damage to cells, tissues, and organs.

MUSCLE MASS

Beginning at age thirty, the body's muscle mass declines by 4 to 6 pounds per decade, and at a higher rate after age sixty. Regular strength training and an adequate protein intake can lessen age-related muscle loss. Healthy protein sources include lean meat, poultry, eggs, soy, milk, fish, beans, legumes, and nuts. For those in the fourth quarter of life, eat protein with every meal and/or snack to maintain muscle mass.

WHAT IS MORE IMPORTANT—
WEIGHT LOSS OR EATING HEALTHY?

Many clients come to my counseling sessions looking for guidance on similar issues. For my fourth-quarter clients, I believe the focus should not be on weight loss, but on eating healthy and moving more. If you carry extra weight, it might drop slowly by focusing on a healthy eating plan—such as the Mediterranean pattern, DASH (dietary approaches to stop hypertension), or the MIND (Mediterranean-DASH intervention for neurodegenerative delay) diet—while also reducing sugar intake and making physical activity a fun part of daily life. And what follows is most often feeling better.

For my fourth-quarter clients, I believe the focus should not be on weight loss, but on eating healthy and moving more.

These three eating patterns have similarities in that the emphasis is on whole, mostly plant-based foods such as nuts, seeds, lentils, soy products, vegetables, fruits, whole grains, lean meat, fish, eggs, and extra virgin olive oil. At the same time, they limit or avoid sweets, red and processed meats, and highly processed snack foods.

As an alternative to the DASH or MIND diets, clients may be prescribed a semaglutide medication for weight loss, which works by suppressing appetite, slowing gastric emptying, and increasing a sense of fullness. A healthy diet is critical in this case because of the possibility of rapid weight loss and insufficient nutrient intake—including vitamins, minerals, protein, healthy fats, and fiber. Some people may have spent years on Metformin, used to lower blood sugar by improving insulin's ability to carry glucose from the blood into body cells for energy. Clients need to know which foods to limit and which foods to increase when taking Metformin. In some cases, slow weight loss combined with a low-sugar diet may improve blood sugar and insulin action enough to where a doctor might lower the Metformin dose or even consider discontinuation.

As stated earlier in this chapter, any questions about concerns, diet plans, exercise, or medication should be directed to your medical professional. My input as a dietitian, hopefully, will trigger your desire to learn more about your health and options by pursuing a meeting(s) with your medical professionals to explore the best options for your care.

LETTERS TO OUR FAVORITE DIETITIAN AND COLUMNIST: LYNNE

The format I chose to present health scenarios is fictional. I present myself as a columnist answering letters from readers to create interest, although my responses are sound and worthy of follow-up with your medical doctor or licensed dietitian. I've chosen these questions because they are common, and you may be experiencing one or more of these yourself.

Health Scenarios by Topic

1. Food and Medication: Navigating Interactions Safely

For readers managing prescriptions, supplements, and chronic conditions.

- **Letter #1** – *Retired and Recharging in Reno*
  → Concerned about interactions between spicy foods, supplements, and meds for blood pressure and anxiety
- **Letter #3** – *Caregiver on the Clock*
  → On cholesterol meds with a hectic caregiving schedule and poor meal timing
- **Letter #8** – *Veteran on the Move*
  → Limited mobility, depends on convenience foods, concerned about salt, and food-drug reactions
- **Letter #14** – *Sunset Years and Still Struggling*
  → Former smoker with chronic obstructive airways disease (COPD); struggling with appetite and energy

2. Managing Health Conditions Through Diet

For readers balancing nutrition with chronic illness, energy, and physical wellness

- **Letter #2** – *Sweet but Struggling*
  → Enjoys sweets but is experiencing joint pain and decreased mobility
- **Letter #5** – *Fruit Lover with Questions*
  → Curious about sugar in fruit as a prediabetic
- **Letter #6** – *Potluck with Purpose*
  → Loves church potlucks but is managing rising cholesterol
- **Letter #7** – *Grandma on the Go*
  → Active and sociable, but newly diagnosed prediabetic

- **Letter #9** – *Bone-Strong Brenda*
  → Recently diagnosed with osteoporosis, wants guidance on food and exercise
- **Letter #16** – *Active but Not Finished at Sixty-Four*
  → Prostate cancer runs in the family, so does poor diet
- **Letter #17** – *Sensitive and Losing Weight*
  → Metastatic breast cancer comes with treatment, but also sensitivity to cosmetics and food

3. Special Populations and Life Transitions

For readers facing unique life stages: pregnancy, solo living, or loss

- **Letter #4** – *Expecting Gracefully*
  → Pregnant at fifty-one, wants guidance on safe foods and prenatal nutrition
- **Letter #11** – *Widowed but Wary*
  → Recently widowed, low appetite, unintended weight loss
- **Letter #12** – *Living Solo and Staying Sharp*
  → Living independently and looking to preserve cognitive health through diet

4. Spirit, Discipline, and Purposeful Eating

For readers looking to integrate their faith with food, fasting, and lifestyle

- **Letter #13** – *Faithful and Fasting*
  → Diabetic seeking to fast for spiritual reasons without harming his health
- **Letter #15** – *Planning with Purpose*
  → Planning for the end of life with a desire for peace and intentional living through dietary choices

5. Relationship Dynamics and Shared Lifestyle Change

For readers navigating changes alongside loved ones

- **Letter #10** – *Two Peas, Different Pods*
  → A couple with different levels of motivation for healthy eating, seeking balance and teamwork

Letters to Our Favorite Dietitian and Columnist: Lynne

Letter #1: From "Retired and Recharging in Reno" (James, 62)

Former police officer, recently started medication for blood pressure and anxiety

Dear Lynne,

I've just retired and was recently prescribed medication for high blood pressure and anxiety. I've always loved spicy food, a good steak on the grill, and the occasional supplement from the vitamin store.

How do I know which foods or supplements could interact badly with my medications? I want to stay healthy, but I also don't want to give up everything I enjoy.

— *Retired and Recharging in Reno*

Letter #1 Reply

Pharmacists are excellent sources of information specific to the medication you are taking, including foods to avoid. In general, alcohol should be avoided, as well as caffeine and St. John's Wort.

If you are taking an MAOI (monoamine oxidase inhibitor) medication—a class of antidepressants—for anxiety, you should avoid aged and fermented foods, beer, and red wine as these can cause a spike in blood pressure, which can be serious.

Grapefruit and grapefruit juice may need to be avoided with both of your medications. Talk to your pharmacist about all the supplements you are taking because these can interfere with prescription medications and other supplements. And make sure you provide your primary care provider with a list of all supplements you are taking.

You should be able to enjoy an occasional steak or other fresh red meat up to 16 oz, or three portions per week, but try to include more plant foods as well. The DASH diet has been shown to improve blood pressure in a majority of people because it is low in salt and added sugar, and higher in potassium, magnesium, and calcium. It is also high in fruits and vegetables, whole grains, low-fat dairy, lean meat, fish, and healthy fats.

Herbs, spices, garlic, onion, lemon, or other citrus juice can be used to create delicious flavor in place of salt.

Letter #2: From "Sweet but Struggling" (Linda, 71)

Widowed, lives alone, loves sweets but has joint pain and limited activity

Dear Lynne,

I've always had a sweet tooth, and now that I'm alone, dessert has become my comfort. My doctor wants me to cut back on sugar, but I don't want to feel deprived. Are there healthier ways to satisfy cravings and still take care of my body, especially with arthritis starting to slow me down?

— *Sweet but Struggling*

Letter #2 Reply

Your doctor is providing preventive care by monitoring your blood sugar in an effort to prevent diabetes, inflammation, or other chronic illnesses. A hemoglobin A1C or HgbA1C result represents your previous 2–3 months of blood sugars. Discuss with your healthcare provider what the goals are for your glucose and HgbA1C , and what they are currently.

As we age, our risk for diabetes increases. Take advantage of this preventive care and start by eliminating fruit juice, candy, regular soda, honey, jams, jellies, and pancake syrup. Eat whole fruit to replace juice, such as berries, kiwi, watermelon, cantaloupe, citrus, and peaches, which are lower in natural sugar.

You can try natural Stevia or monk fruit to sweeten foods without using sugar or adding calories. Then reduce the frequency of your dessert intake, such as every other day instead of daily. After you achieve this goal, take the challenge even further to eat a single dessert only once a week. Plan to eat some of your meals with friends, family, or community to provide comfort rather than getting comfort from sweets. It's not easy to cut back on foods you love, but setting achievable, stepwise goals is helpful. Taking a short ten-minute walk after eating can improve blood sugar levels, as well as walking each day or adding strength-training exercises. Master one goal at a time before moving on to the next goal.

Check with your doctor to monitor your improved blood values after these changes to guide further sugar intake modifications. This may be all you need to achieve your goals. You will likely feel better and motivated to stick with these changes!

Letter #3 – "Caregiver on the Clock" (Monique, 63)

On cholesterol meds with a hectic caregiving schedule and poor meal timing

Dear Lynne,

Between work and caring for my aging parents, my meals are unpredictable. I'll sometimes go for hours without eating, then grab fast food late at night.

I've recently started a new cholesterol medication. Is there a risk in skipping meals or eating erratically while on it? How can I make better food choices without a big lifestyle change?

— *Caregiver on the Clock*

Letter #3 Reply

You have a lot on your plate, so to speak! It's a good sign that you are concerned about inconsistent meals and want to make better food choices because you need to care for yourself to have the energy and stamina to continue all your caregiving responsibilities. It will require more meal planning than you have done in the past.

Using partially prepared ingredients can save a lot of time. These include proteins, such as chopped precooked chicken breast, rotisserie chicken, premade meatballs, sliced or shredded cheese, frozen shrimp, pre-portioned salmon, or sliced nuts. Also, choosing chopped fresh vegetables, chopped frozen fruit, precooked beets, chopped garlic, chopped ginger, and chopped basil can save time. Smoothies can be quickly made using frozen fruit, sliced nuts, granola, yogurt, and chia seeds.

Choose a block of time, such as the weekend, to do batch meal preparation for the week. A batch of Spanish rice can be divided so that 1–2 servings at a time can be heated and mixed with vegetables and meat for a quick meal. Pre-packaged green salads or fresh chopped vegetables are ready quickly after roasting in the oven or steaming.

Crockpots or slow cookers are great for putting the ingredients in before work and finishing by the time you arrive home from work. Instant pots have become extremely popular because a complete meal is ready in a fraction of the usual cooking time.

Letter #4: From "Expecting Gracefully" (Jasmine, 51)

Pregnant later in life, wants to stay healthy and informed

Dear Lynne,

At fifty-one, I find myself joyfully—yet cautiously—pregnant. With this being a high-risk pregnancy, I'm doing all I can to be careful. What foods should I be avoiding entirely while pregnant, especially as someone approaching her fourth quarter of life? Are there specific interactions between prenatal vitamins and foods I should watch for?

— *Expecting Gracefully*

Letter #4 Reply

The primary reason for avoiding supplements or medications while taking prenatal vitamins (PNV) is that the existing medications decrease their absorption or interact with them. These medications and foods shouldn't be consumed within two hours of taking PNV—antacids, thyroid medication, calcium, anti-seizure drugs, coffee and tea, milk, and other dairy products. Avoid herbal supplements, as some of them are considered unsafe during pregnancy.

Foods to avoid during pregnancy include raw fish or seafood such as sushi or sashimi, big eye tuna, swordfish, shark, tilefish, mackerel, orange roughy, and marlin. Also, avoid alcohol, raw milk, unpasteurized milk, or juices. Heat deli meat or hot dogs until hot and avoid undercooked meat, eggs, and poultry. Minimal caffeine is okay. Eating 8–12 oz of a variety of seafood is recommended if desired, providing beneficial omega-3 fatty acids for fetal brain development.

Letter #5: From "Fruit Lover with Questions" (Deborah, 67)

Prediabetic and confused about the sugar content of fruit

Dear Lynne,

I've been told to watch my sugars, but no one explained how fruit fits into that. I eat apples, bananas, and grapes daily, and I've recently added smoothies to my routine. Are fruits too sugary for someone watching their blood sugar levels? How can I enjoy fruit without risking spikes?

— *Fruit Lover with Questions*

Letter #5 Reply

I am so glad you reached out for clarification of the unclear message to watch your sugars. It is good for your healthcare provider to monitor your blood sugar, but it is important to know just how to do it, since we have an increased risk of diabetes as we age. You need direction and specific practical steps to take. Ask your medical provider what your fasting glucose and HgbA1C goals are, and then track your progress.

Inactivity and being overweight are factors that can cause a higher-than-normal blood sugar level. Just a short ten-minute walk after eating can have an impact on lowering blood glucose levels. Added sugars and refined carbohydrates, which are prevalent in convenience foods and baked foods, become glucose when digested and metabolized by the body.

As a start to reducing your blood glucose level, I recommend eliminating foods with the highest concentration of sugar and the lowest nutrient level, such as candy, soda, pancake syrup, honey, jam, and jelly. Use the natural sweetener Stevia or monk fruit, which tastes sweet but has no sugar or calories, to substitute for sugar in foods or beverages you consume frequently. Avoid desserts most days.

Fruit is a nutritious food full of vitamins, minerals, and fiber required to optimize health, digestion, and metabolism. Some fruits have less fructose or natural fruit sugar than others, such as peaches, berries, watermelon, cantaloupe, kiwi, and citrus. A recommended serving is half a cup or a small-sized piece of fruit, such as an orange or one cup of berries. To avoid spikes in blood sugar, I recommend eating a serving of fruit with a protein food to slow digestion and moderate glucose metabolism.

During your follow-up appointment with your physician, scheduled a few months after detecting high glucose levels, it is advisable to undergo additional laboratory tests to assess the effectiveness of your dietary and lifestyle modifications. The changes I recommended above should make a significant difference if you stick with them, but if you need to lower your glucose further, you may have to consider reducing your intake of carbohydrate foods to make a bigger impact on lowering your blood sugar levels. Contact a local dietitian for help at eatright.org.

Letter #6: From "Potluck with Purpose" (Naomi, 74)

African American woman, deeply involved in her church and its food-centered gatherings

Dear Lynne,

I love our church potlucks, especially the soul food I grew up with. But my doctor says my cholesterol is creeping up, and I'm worried about my heart. How can I still enjoy our gatherings and honor my culture without hurting my health?

— *Potluck with Purpose*

Letter #6 Reply

I encourage you to continue to honor your cultural food traditions while enjoying your potluck gatherings at church. During this quarter of your life, keep in mind that food is not only a source of energy and nutrients but also a source of enjoyment when shared with those in your community, whom you care about.

Your medical concerns require adjustments in your eating choices, and daily exercise can also have a positive impact on cholesterol. Cholesterol levels are driven somewhat by genetics, which we have no control over, and by diet, which we can control by decreasing our intake of saturated fat. This type of fat comes from animal foods such as meat, processed meat, butter, lard, cheese, full-fat dairy products used in bakery products, coconut and palm oil, and fried foods. Processed foods should be limited. Trans fats are even unhealthier than saturated fats, but they have been banned by the Food and Drug Administration (FDA) for use in processed foods since 2020.

The Mediterranean diet emphasizes eating seafood, lean meat, fruits and vegetables, seeds, nuts, legumes, olive oil, and whole grains, and it's an excellent framework to guide our food choices. Soluble fiber, such as oats or oatmeal, barley, beans, apples, and pears, can lower cholesterol by preventing the absorption of cholesterol in the gut.

Lifestyle emphasis is on daily exercise—of a minimum of thirty minutes of moderate activity—to maintain a healthy weight, lose excess weight, and, if needed, lower cholesterol. Practicing this eating pattern at home and then, as you are able, at the potlucks, can have a positive impact without taking the joy out of savoring your cultural preferences with a collection of your favorite people. If, after several months of minimizing your saturated fat intake most days, there is no improvement in your cholesterol, you may want to try an omega-3 supplement in addition to continuing your lifestyle and nutrition changes. Consult your healthcare provider or dietitian for specific recommendations.

Letter #7: From "Grandma on the Go" (Charlene, 63)

Pre-diabetic, active, enjoys socializing and wine

Dear Lynne,

I love staying active and spending time with my grandkids. I'm also a huge fan of tasty food and the occasional glass of wine with friends. But now I'm told I'm pre-diabetic. What small, realistic changes can I make so I don't feel like I'm giving up all the joys of life?

— *Grandma on the Go*

Letter #7 Reply

Yes, there are small, realistic changes you can make without having to give up on the joys of your life! Prediabetes needs to be taken seriously, so take action soon to avoid diabetes requiring medication, and avoid the damage and chronic inflammation that high blood sugar can cause.

Since fruit is a carbohydrate that metabolizes quickly into glucose, make sure to eat fruit with a protein such as cheese, meat or poultry, egg, nuts, or a whey protein shake. Berries, watermelon, cantaloupe, kiwi, peaches, and citrus are a few of the fruits lower in fructose or fruit sugar. Avoid foods with high sugar content and low nutrient content, such as jam, jelly, honey, pancake syrup, soda, and candy. Highly processed foods such as crackers and baked goods are high in carbohydrates, so choose these products less often.

Make an effort to eat more vegetables with every meal to replace a serving of rice, potatoes, or bread, which are all carbohydrates. A variety of beans is a good carbohydrate choice because beans are high in fiber, which slows digestion, including the digestion of carbohydrates. You mentioned wine is something you enjoy in social settings, and you can continue to enjoy it. There is an exceedingly small amount of carbohydrate in wine, which makes it a fine choice. A 5-oz glass contains 5 grams of carbohydrate. But as with anything, it is possible to overdo it.

You can also take a ten-minute walk after your meal to increase the uptake of glucose by body cells. In addition, make sure to get physical activity for a minimum of thirty minutes daily, at least five days a week. Walking is a viable choice for most people, and there are many other forms of exercise available too. It's important to do something you enjoy so you have a better chance of continuing with it. If you don't enjoy it, you will lose interest and give up.

These small practical changes should have a substantial impact, so check with your healthcare provider in a couple of months to find out your progress in lowering your blood glucose and hemoglobin A1C values! If you need to count how many carbohydrates you are eating at each meal—to affect your blood sugar more deliberately—contact a dietitian in your area through eatright.org, or check with your local hospital to see if they have outpatient nutrition counseling provided by a dietitian.

Letter #8: From "Veteran on the Move" (Don, 76)

Vietnam veteran with limited mobility, eats frozen and canned meals

Dear Lynne,

My mobility is limited these days, so I rely on what I can heat up quickly—mostly canned or frozen food. I'm also on several prescriptions, including a blood thinner. Should I be concerned about salt or other ingredients in these meals clashing with my meds? What minor changes can I make to avoid food-drug conflicts?

— *Veteran on the Move*

Letter #8 Reply

First of all, I thank you and appreciate your service to our country.

For quick and easy menu items, use frozen fruit for smoothies and add plain Greek yogurt, kefir, or whey protein. Old-fashioned oats can be cooked for a single serving in the microwave and provide soluble fiber, which is beneficial for a healthy gut, regularity, and lower cholesterol. Big box stores like Sam's Club or Costco have several frozen seafood options, some of which are packaged in a serving or portion size. Herbs, lemon, spices, spice mixes, balsamic vinegar, olive oil, soy sauce, teriyaki sauce, butter, garlic, and onion add good flavor. Minced garlic, chopped ginger and basil, chopped onion, and bell pepper can be purchased either frozen or from the shelf.

Choose pre-roasted poultry and chunk light tuna for quick protein meals. You can also buy roasted and chopped chicken to add to a salad, or heat and add to pasta or rice. Canned chicken breast is a good choice for adding to soup or making chicken salad sandwiches. Canned beans or refried beans can make a quick meal, such as tacos or tostadas with a pre-shredded cheese, shredded lettuce, pre-chopped onion, and a jar of salsa. Rinsing canned beans removes most of the sodium, which is a prevalent ingredient in canned products.

Fresh or frozen vegetables are quick to heat up and are better than canned. There are many options now for premade salad mixes, chopped fresh vegetables, and ready-to-eat salads to provide necessary fiber, vitamins, and minerals.

If you are taking warfarin, you need to avoid foods high in vitamin K, such as kale, spinach, parsley, brussels sprouts, cabbage, and Swiss chard. Minimal amounts of these foods are okay, for example, as a small serving as part of a salad, but large amounts should be avoided. Fish oil supplements and St. John's Wort should be avoided as well. Some of the newer blood thinners do not have food-drug interactions. Ask your healthcare provider if one of these blood thinners would be appropriate for you.

As you age, you lose skeletal muscle, so it is important to eat more protein than you did when younger, as well as do strength training to maintain muscle mass. Since muscle is essential to mobility, aim to do what you can to maintain the mobility you have. Having a protein serving with each meal is a general guideline, and then supplementing with homemade protein shakes or purchased protein shakes can help meet your needs. Protein foods are eggs, lean meat, fish, dairy products, beans, peas, lentils, quinoa, soy products, nuts, and seeds.

Letter #9: From "Bone-Strong Brenda" (Brenda, 59)

Recently diagnosed with osteoporosis, wants guidance on food and exercise

Dear Lynne,

I've just been diagnosed with osteoporosis, and I want to take the right steps before it gets worse. I'm still working and enjoy gentle yoga and walking. What foods help my bones stay strong? And are there certain movements or supplements I should avoid?

— *Bone-Strong Brenda*

Letter #9 Reply

Diet and exercise are important, beneficial, and supportive measures for osteoporosis, even though it has a strong genetic component. Any weight-bearing physical activity is crucial to bone density. In addition to yoga and walking, other options include tai chi, running, hiking, dancing, aerobics, and strength training. The recommendation is for a minimum of thirty minutes daily or 150 minutes per week.

Calcium requirement increases by age sixty as bone density decreases with age and post menopause. Women aged fifty and older need 1,200 mg daily to slow bone mineral loss. Foods such as dairy products, dark green leafy vegetables, and calcium-fortified products such as orange juice, milk beverages, and soy milk are good sources, but most often, supplements are needed to meet the daily recommended amount of calcium. There are different forms of calcium supplements, one of which is calcium citrate, which can be taken with or without meals and is usually the better choice if you have low stomach acid or inflammatory bowel disease.

Vitamin D is needed for calcium absorption, and it is difficult to get entirely from foods in your diet, such as fortified milk and milk beverages, orange juice, cereals, salmon, tuna, trout, herring, sardines, eggs, and beef liver. The recommended intake is 600 IU (international units) for people up to seventy years of age and 800 IU for those over seventy years of age. A simple blood test can show if you are getting the right amount of vitamin D, and a physician-ordered dual-energy X-ray absorptiometry (DEXA) scan can show bone density.

Letter #10: From "Two Peas, Different Pods" (Sam and Deborah, 69 and 67)

A married couple trying to eat better together, with different levels of motivation

Dear Lynne,

My wife is all in on a healthy eating plan. Me? Not so much. I like what I like, and change isn't easy. We want to make changes together, but it's becoming a bit of a tug-of-war. How can couples work together on better eating habits without driving each other nuts?

— *Two Peas, Different Pods*

Letter #10 Reply

Start by clarifying what you each want to achieve and then collaborate on how to get there. It may take compromise from each of you to be successful, but the reward will be worth it! It also takes time for old habits to change. Start with a small, achievable habit to conquer before moving on to more difficult habits. Be encouraging and supportive to one another as you replace old habits with healthier, more constructive ones.

Hopefully, you agree with a pattern of eating that will provide lots of choices and variety so that you will have options you both enjoy. You may want to start with the Mediterranean eating pattern, which is not only a healthy way to eat but is also a lifestyle that supports health. It promotes daily physical activity and enjoying meals with others.

Be creative, laugh together, and work as a team to lighten the stress load. Try new recipes that you agree with. Decide together on something fun to do to reward yourselves when you reach the final goal of your step-by-step process.

Letter #11: From "Widowed and Wary" (Howard, 78)

Lost his spouse of fifty years, recently began eating less and losing weight

Dear Lynne,

Since my wife passed away, I don't have much of an appetite. Cooking for one just isn't the same. I've lost weight without meaning to, and I'm starting to feel weaker. What can I do to keep my nutrition up when I don't feel like eating? Is this normal grief, or should I be concerned? I've started drinking nutritional supplement drinks, but I'm concerned that these drinks are not sufficient as a regular diet.

— *Widowed and Wary*

Letter #11 Reply

You have experienced a big life change in losing your spouse and companion for so many years. It's not unusual to feel the way you do, and the period of grieving is different for everyone. If there is a senior community center near you, I recommend looking into it—they offer low-cost meals in a community setting.

Oftentimes, that alone can improve your appetite. Reach out to family and friends and join them for a meal. Eating small, frequent meals can be beneficial when your appetite is diminished. It isn't as difficult to eat a small meal as it is to eat a larger one.

Protein supplement drinks can help with both protein and calorie intake but add small meals or snacks. Check the nutrition label because some of the high-protein supplements are low in calories, and you want one that is high in calories. They are called supplements because they supplement your regular meals rather than replace them. Depending on your needs, one to three 8–12-ounce drinks per day can be helpful. Protein and calories are both important because if your calorie (energy) intake is too low, your body will burn protein for energy rather than use it to build and maintain muscle mass and other bodily functions. Muscle is protein, and muscle keeps you mobile and active.

Daily walks are excellent to keep you moving rather than being sedentary and becoming stiff and weak. You may enjoy other activities such as dancing, tennis, lawn games, tai chi, or bowling.

Look for partially prepared meal ingredients like frozen fruit, cooked chicken, chopped vegetables, mixed salads, and pre-portioned fish. Tuna, eggs, cottage cheese, and fruit are quick to prepare, as are sandwiches, smoothies, and milkshakes. There are healthy options for frozen meals that are not high in salt. Be sure to include your favorite dishes and eat a variety of fruits and vegetables, whole grains, and salads.

Letter #12: From "Living Solo and Staying Sharp" (Margie, 65)

Living independently, wants to stay mentally sharp and avoid cognitive decline

Dear Lynne,

I live alone and am mostly independent, but I'm starting to forget small things—names, appointments, where I put my keys. I want to do all I can to protect my mind. Are there foods or nutrients that support brain health at my age? Or is it just about crossword puzzles and sleep?

— *Living Solo and Staying Sharp*

Letter #12 Reply

I will briefly describe the MIND diet, or eating plan, which is designed to diminish cognitive decline. It is anti-inflammatory, rich in antioxidants, and provides necessary nutrients for optimal nutrition. It is a combination of the Mediterranean and DASH diets. It is both brain and heart healthy, particularly due to the focus on eating fish weekly and eating mostly whole plant foods. Omega-3 fatty acid research links fish—especially fatty fish such as salmon, herring, sardines, trout, and tuna—to a reduced risk of cognitive decline. The serving recommendation for fish is 4 oz one or more times per week. A 3-oz portion of chicken or turkey is recommended two or more times per week.

Whole plant foods include vegetables, fruits, whole grains, olive oil, nuts, seeds, and legumes such as beans and lentils, along with protein-rich foods like fish, eggs, and lean meats. Some of the most nutrient-dense choices are berries, beets, walnuts, pumpkin seeds, legumes, and leafy greens. Eating foods in a variety of colors gives you plenty of phytonutrients (plant compounds), which work together to deliver the powerful benefits of phytonutrients.

The recommended servings of whole grains, such as oats, bulgur, farro, barley, brown rice, whole wheat bread, and quinoa (a complete protein food), are three daily. One cup of berries of all types should be consumed twice weekly. Nuts provide healthy fats, minerals—such as magnesium, potassium, and zinc—vitamin E, B vitamins, and fiber. It is recommended to have five 1-oz servings per week of nuts (approximately twenty-five almonds). Olive oil should be the primary oil for cooking while minimizing the use of butter or margarine.

Leafy greens are rich in plant compounds. Try to eat six or more servings per week. The most common greens are lettuce, spinach, kale, arugula, cabbage, bok choy, swiss chard, brussels sprouts, watercress, and collard greens. Include other vegetables at least once daily in addition to the leafy greens. Choose a variety of colors.

Beans, lentils, and soybeans are fiber rich and help control blood glucose, provide fiber for a healthy gut microbiome, and slow digestion, giving a sense of fullness and satiety. A serving size is half a cup, recommended four times or more per week.

Foods that should be avoided or limited are:

- Fried foods, especially prepared from fast-food restaurants.
- Processed snack foods, pastries, sweets, and desserts up to only four times weekly.
- Red meat should be limited to three servings weekly.
- Cheese should be eaten less than once weekly.

Letter #13: From "Faithful and Fasting" (Elijah, 62)

Practicing intermittent fasting for spiritual and health reasons, also diabetic

Dear Lynne,

I've been experimenting with intermittent fasting as part of my prayer and health routine. I'm also a diabetic, and I want to be careful not to cause harm while trying to do good. What's the best way to fast safely with my condition? Are there specific foods I should eat when fasting?

— Faithful and Fasting

Letter #13 Reply

Fasting for spiritual reasons can be an important practice in one's faith. If you have Type 1 diabetes, you should not fast. Intermittent fasting is cycling specific time frames during the day, either in an eight-hour, ten-hour, or twelve-hour window to eat, and fasting the remaining hours every day. The main health benefits are that it lowers blood glucose and circulating insulin levels and has the potential to lessen inflammation.

If you have Type 2 diabetes and you are taking oral medication such as Metformin, the sixteen-hour fast overnight with eight hours during the day for all meals and snacks is the best schedule. Be sure to stay well hydrated. The types of foods eaten are important for diabetics so that glucose doesn't have a steep rise and then fall when fasting begins. Make sure to eat more protein and fewer carbohydrates to help blood sugar remain steady.

The types of carbohydrate which are better for the body are vegetables, berries, complex high-fiber carbohydrates—such as whole grains, beans, lentils. Include healthy fats, including avocado and nuts; low-fat dairy such as kefir and Greek or regular yogurt with no added sugar. Avoid sugary foods, sweets, desserts, or highly processed foods such as snack foods and bakery products or cereals that are not whole grain. For the fasting period, water and clear coffee or tea are allowed.

Letter #14: From "Sunset Years and Still Struggling" (Gloria, 70)

Former smoker with COPD, struggling with breathing, low appetite, and fatigue

Dear Lynne,

I quit smoking five years ago, but I have COPD now and it's wearing me down. I don't eat much because breathing takes so much energy. Are there foods that can help me breathe easier or give me strength without filling me up too much?

— *Sunset Years and Still Struggling*

Letter #14 Reply

It is particularly challenging to eat enough to maintain your weight with a chronic illness such as COPD due to difficulty breathing when eating. It is especially important for you to choose foods with high nutrient density, which means maximum nutrients per serving of food. Foods such as sugary desserts and sweets, bakery products, highly processed crackers, and chips are to be eaten rarely, possibly even saved for special occasions, since they have no healthy nutrient value.

I recommend eating three small meals and 2–3 snacks as needed daily. Your meal should begin with high-quality protein so that you do not get full prior to eating this essential nutrient. These foods are fish, lean poultry, eggs, fermented dairy—like plain yogurt, plain Greek yogurt, and cottage cheese—and seafood. Fruit or berries can be added to some of these foods to make them sweeter or combined to make a smoothie to which whey protein is added. Protein shakes can be purchased for use as a snack for ease and to increase calories and nutrients. Quinoa looks like a grain but is actually a seed and is a whole protein food. It is light and can be added to a salad or mixed with vegetables and herbs or spices for a healthy choice. Also, try sipping small amounts of liquid at a time, preferably between meals, so you don't fill up while you're trying to eat more food.

Whole grains, legumes, avocado, and nuts can be added to salads with olive oil and vinegar or lemon dressing. As a general guideline, the Mediterranean eating plan can be used when creating your menus. When possible, share a meal with friends or family so you can stay connected with loved ones.

Limit salt, processed foods, red meat, and saturated fat in addition to sweets and processed foods, as described above. A multivitamin and mineral for your age and gender would be of benefit. Vegetables and fruit provide many vitamins and minerals, but they are so filling that you may not be able to eat as many as you need. Seek meal planning advice and recipes from a registered dietitian at eatright.org to optimize your limited food intake.

Talk with your healthcare provider to see which calcium and vitamin D supplements would best meet your needs since you are highly likely to be deficient in these nutrients. Take the calcium at a separate time from the multivitamin to avoid absorption conflicts.

Letter #15: From "Planning with Purpose"
(Douglas, 80)

Recently updated his will and advance directives, wants to align health choices with planning

Dear Lynne,

I've been thinking more about the end of life lately and have made plans for my estate and care wishes. Now I want to make healthy choices that reflect my values: living well but not obsessing over adding years. What does a balanced, faith-informed approach to diet and wellness look like when your goal is peace, not perfection?

— *Planning with Purpose*

Letter #15 Reply

This is an insightful question about how you want to enjoy quality time while living with purpose during your fourth quarter of life. Healthy nutrition and wellness can be taken to an extreme, which is a perspective that almost makes an idol out of it, and loses sight of the joys in life—such as celebrating those relationships that mean the most to us, loving God and others, living out our faith in a meaningful way, and finding peace and fulfillment.

You have to ask yourself what is most important at this stage of your life, and then what the other priorities are that you want to focus on. Health and wellness are supporting factors to be mindful of because you feel better, have more energy, and have better cognitive function when you prioritize these aspects of your life. Being willing to do your best with healthy nutrition, sleep, and exercise in order to change what you can allows you to focus on what is most important—loving your family, friends, and God. What you choose to devote yourself to takes time, and time is your most valuable resource because you will not get more of it.

Letter #16: From "Active but Not Finished" (Leon, 64)

Leon has been very active his entire life, but his family history includes cancer, and now he needs treatment and a dietary change

Dear Lynne,

I've always been very active in sports, travel, and the epicurean lifestyle. So, I look at my recent diagnosis of prostate cancer as a challenge to conquer, which I will. But I have also come to grips with my weight. What in particular should I change as I go through treatment and then emerge to become healthier through diet—both short and long term?

— *Active but Not Finished*

Letter #16 Reply

I will cover the nutrition-related symptoms that you might experience through treatment, which could be either radiation or androgen deprivation therapy (ADT), and how to manage them. Two of the most beneficial interventions for you will be regular exercise and a low-fiber diet.

You mention that you are overweight. If possible, decrease your weight slowly during treatment. Losing weight too quickly during treatment can increase the risk of treatment breaks or even discontinuation. If slow weight loss during treatment is not possible, plan to lose weight after treatment to reduce the risk of recurrence of the disease. Instead, aim to maintain your weight and prioritize protein intake to preserve muscle mass and protect against bone loss.

Protein is important for maintaining muscle. Aim to eat about 1.2 to 1.5 grams of protein per kilogram of body weight each day. To find your weight in kilograms, divide your weight in pounds by 2.2. Then multiply that number by 1.2 to 1.5 to determine your daily protein target. Try to spread this intake evenly throughout the day. A whey protein shake can help build muscle, especially when combined with exercise. Stay active by walking daily and add in strength exercises 2–3 times a week if you can. For bone health, include calcium-rich foods and vitamin D—most people need around 1,000–1,200 mg of calcium and 600 IU of vitamin D daily.

For digestion issues like diarrhea, which can happen during radiation, a low-fat, low-fiber diet can help, along with any medications your doctor recommends. Some people also find probiotics helpful. For heart health, consider the National Heart Association's diet guidelines, which focus on whole grains, fruits, vegetables, and healthy fats. You might also need to watch your carbohydrate intake, especially if your blood sugar runs high. It can also help to cut back on things like caffeine, hot drinks, alcohol, spicy foods, and smoking.

For long-term health after treatment, aim for at least thirty minutes of moderate activity each day, or three or more hours of vigorous exercise each week. Staying active helps recovery and overall well-being.

When it comes to food, certain foods are more supportive of your health. Include tomatoes (cooked or raw), guava, and watermelon, cruciferous vegetables—like broccoli, cauliflower, and Brussels sprouts—leafy greens, soy foods, egg whites, unprocessed poultry without the skin, two servings of fish per week, and low-fat or nonfat dairy products. Try to limit foods like baked goods, poultry skin, red and processed meats, whole-milk dairy products, and heavily processed meals.

These changes can help support heart health, maintain a healthy weight, and reduce your risk of recurrence. Start small and build healthy habits over time—you don't have to do it all at once.

Letter #17: From "Sensitive and Losing Weight" (Destiny, 54)

Destiny was first diagnosed with breast cancer at age forty-nine. Now she is diagnosed with metastatic breast cancer; it has metastasized to her bones. The sensitivity of her skin to cosmetics and clothing (roughness) is a challenge, but so is her food sensitivity.

Dear Lynne,

I am the first in our family with breast cancer, now metastatic breast cancer. I'm finding the sensitivity to cosmetics and clothing irritating. I now need everything near my skin to be ultra soft. My bigger problem is diet! With ongoing chemotherapy, my appetite is also struggling, hence my rapid weight loss. What should my diet consist of to complement my treatment and to combat weight loss?

— *Sensitive and Losing Weight*

Letter #17 Reply

Let's address your biggest problem first—your diet. One of the biggest challenges during chemotherapy is a loss of appetite, which can lead to rapid weight loss. This is often made worse by other side effects of treatment, such as mouth sores, nausea, vomiting, fatigue, or changes in taste, which can all make eating difficult.

It might help to consider food as medicine for now instead of something you enjoy. Even small amounts of nutritional food can help you maintain some weight and support your healing. Seek a registered or licensed dietitian if you are losing more than 1–2 pounds per week. They can help you find foods and create meal plans that are bearable.

Eating small, frequent meals and snacks 6–8 times a day can increase your calorie intake. Eat nutrient-dense foods, so you get a high nutrient level per volume. Use supplements such as protein shakes or make smoothies with whey protein powder to increase protein intake. Drink fluids between meals. Use foods that are easy to prepare. Keep a variety of these foods in your kitchen because when you are undergoing treatment, your desire for certain foods is fickle, and you can change your mind quickly!

If you are taking an aromatase inhibitor, increase your physical activity if possible, especially weight-bearing exercises. Take 1,200 mg of calcium daily for bone health, and a vitamin D supplement if your physician says your serum levels are below 20–30 ng/mL

Regarding the many side effects of chemotherapy, anti-nausea therapy, acupressure, and acupuncture can help with nausea and vomiting. For mouth sores, some studies recommend glutamine 2.5 grams as a swish and swallow three times daily for fourteen days. Walking for short periods a few times a day can keep food moving through your gastrointestinal (GI) tract.

Many patients receiving treatment for breast cancer gain weight, so it is important to be aware of this possibility since it is usually an unwanted side effect that recurs. In the long term, it is recommended to maintain a normal weight and exercise for thirty minutes daily most days.

At times when your skin is sensitive, usually from radiation or chemo, cool bath soaks with baking soda, oatmeal, or oil can be soothing. Soft, loose clothing is more comfortable. Use an unscented therapeutic lotion such as Eucerin Advanced Repair

Lotion to keep your skin moist. Avoiding cosmetics as much as possible may also help reduce your skin sensitivity.

———

If Lynne's words have spoken to you—as they did to me—take them to heart. Let this be your nudge to begin. Start small. Start today. You are absolutely worth it!

CHAPTER 4

VOCATIONALLY ALIGNED

By Scott Couchenour

THE MOONSHINE PRINCIPLE

I had the pleasure of meeting Scott through a mutual friend. We connected because of common interests and beliefs, but shortly after, our friendship grew to include a potential business arrangement, developing a paid-subscription online platform offering a digital library, opportunities to connect with professionals, chat rooms, and yearly in-person gatherings. This is when I quickly realized and appreciated Scott's strategic approach to business and life, with personal and ethical values that I wanted to be part of.

We continue to talk about our business venture, and hopefully, one day, our vision will be a reality. Until then, it is my pleasure to introduce Scott. I encourage you to read slowly to absorb Scott's wisdom and mentoring because there's immense value to be gleaned.

MY VOCATIONAL MISALIGNMENT

I was fifty years old when I took a call that would change my life forever. I was the CEO of a multi-million-dollar family-owned business that designed and built churches across America. My dad is a preacher's kid. His dad, my grandpa, was going through a building program in the mid-1960s when the contractor inflated the final invoice and skipped town. This left Grandpa without a finished sanctuary and no money to complete the project.

Dad stepped in and obtained the needed financing and got the project completed. In fact, he found the contractor who was in a neighboring state and compelled him to repay the money. After this was all done, my dad was in a conversation over lunch one day, when someone spoke the words that were the origin of our family business: "There ought to be a company that exists to see this doesn't happen to churches anymore."

Dad incorporated in 1970 and began helping one church after another. Soon, he was faced with the decision of whether to ride the horse himself until he was done or grow the business big enough for all five of his children to have the option to join him. He chose the latter, and eventually three of us joined.

We successfully transitioned from the first generation (my dad) to the second generation of two of my brothers and me. Dad was the chairman of the board while the three of us ran the company. All was going well until the financial collapse of 2008. It was the beginning of the end for us, but we didn't realize it until five years later.

In 2013, the board of directors, after five years of declining sales, asked me to assume the role of CEO. I was the chief operating officer (COO) for twenty-four years prior. They gave me one job: reinvent our forty-year-old business. I went to work, and dozens of whiteboards later, an idea cropped up. Based on that, we began restructuring how we were going to approach the market. There was a glimmer of hope among the twelve surviving employees, down from a high of seventy.

However, the five-year decline from 2008 to 2013 had created a cash flow situation. We were maxed out on our line of credit and became exceedingly dependent on one project starting in June of 2015. I was fifty years old. We had $20 million in projects under contract in various stages of design that we were working toward. But this one project had to bridge the gap with cash until that backlog could open up.

I received a call in June of 2015 from the project manager, expecting to hear him say they'd gotten started. Instead, he asked if I was sitting down before he said, "The news of the pastor's affair with the secretary just came out."

I was devastated. This was our last hope. Gone.

Long story short, we closed the business down after forty-four years, 760 projects, and nearly half a million square feet of shelter for worship and ministry. I lost my income, my career, and, most devastatingly, my identity. I was no longer vocationally aligned.

WHAT IS VOCATIONAL ALIGNMENT?

Let's parse the phrase "vocational alignment" to get a better grasp of this hallmark. First, the word "vocational" is typically associated with a job. We expend our time and energy and receive a paycheck as a result. While that's part of the definition, it's not exclusive.

I define "vocation" as whatever you give your time, energy, and attention to. Sometimes it results in a paycheck, ownership, or equity stake. But not always. For example, I get down on the floor with my three-year-old grandson, Wesley, and play with Legos or Matchbox trucks. In that moment, I'm giving Wes my mental, physical, and emotional investment. That's my vocation at that point in time.

This definition is significant because it opens up our minds to think about the bigger picture. From the moment we wake up and become aware of the day until the moment we drift off to sleep, we are giving our resources, focus, and effort to multiple endeavors. For the business owner or executive in a long-term career, most of their waking hours have been spent in one main area. As a result, they think that vocation is just a job. It's not. It's a whole lot more. We'll come back to this concept later when talking about the *moonshine principle.* But let's finish parsing the phrase.

> *From the moment we wake up and become aware of the day until the moment we drift off to sleep, we are giving our time, energy, and attention to multiple endeavors.*

The second word is "alignment." This presumes there is something to which we are in need of aligning. Our lifespan is full of seasons and stages. Seasons come and go. When I broke my left arm, I had to adapt and write with my right hand, not my dominant hand. For a season, my handwriting was horrible. Then, after the cast was removed and I started writing again, my handwriting improved because I was able to use my dominant hand. That's a season. It comes to pass.

Stages, in contrast to seasons, are linear. We enter a stage, progress through it, and come out of the stage when we are done. We never go back to a previous stage. For example, I ran the Pittsburgh marathon when I was in my mid-thirties. I followed a sixteen-week training guidebook entitled *The Non-Runners Mar-*

athon Trainer.[1] It was extremely helpful. It's what got my body and mind in shape to finish the marathon in four hours and thirty-seven minutes—an average of approximately eleven-minute miles. If I were to train for another marathon now, my training would involve a bit more careful consideration. That's because I'm not a man in his thirties anymore, and I never will be. I'm in my sixties now, and that's where I'll be until I reach the next stage of life.

The reason we parse the words "vocational" and "alignment" is that over time, as we progress through seasons and stages, our vocations become misaligned. It's in each stage that we need to consider what needs to be added, deleted, or changed in order to reach a point of alignment.

As we progress through seasons and stages, our vocations become misaligned.

For example, let's say a business owner founded a company over forty years ago. She loved every minute of it—the board meetings, the high-stakes negotiations, and the late-night strategy sessions. Her identity, purpose, and energy were all deeply tied to that work. But then she became a grandmother. A seven-pound newborn suddenly captivated her attention, and she had a new priority. The boardroom didn't sparkle like it once did. She found herself distracted in meetings, thinking more about nursery colors than quarterly projections. That's not burnout, it's the early signal of vocational misalignment.

Vocational misalignment doesn't always begin with frustration. Often, it starts with affection—a shift in what tugs at your

---

[1] David A. Whitsett, Forrest A. Dolgener, and Tanjala Jo Kole, *The Non-Runner's Marathon Trainer* (New York: McGraw-Hill, 1998).

heart. And while the demands of life don't stop, they do shift. What once fit like a glove may now feel like a burden. That's when it's time to pause and reassess.

Vocational misalignment doesn't always begin with frustration. Often, it starts with affection—a shift in what tugs at your heart.

When considering an alignment to your vocation, don't think of it as abandoning responsibility. Think of it like realigning your time, energy, and attention with *what matters most now*. This may involve letting go of certain roles, adjusting commitments, or even redefining success. The goal isn't to recreate what was, *but to move forward into what is* with clarity and intention.

Vocational alignment is dynamic. It evolves. And the wiser we become, the more we recognize that staying aligned takes regular recalibration—not just once at retirement, but throughout our lives.

When we map out a fantastic life, one of the lenses is to be ideally vocationally aligned. This takes adjustment and iteration because life doesn't stand still.

THE MOONSHINE PRINCIPLE

Let's talk about moonshine.

No, I'm not talking about the buzz you get from consuming a certain kind of liquid generated in a distillery that's hidden in a valley between a couple of mountains. Rather, I'm talking about the ocean on a moonlit night.

There's something almost intoxicating about it, but it has nothing to do with alcohol. My wife and I have a rhythm, a kind of sacred ritual, when we're away on a beach vacation. After the sun sets and the noise from the grandkids and the events of the day subside, we find ourselves drawn to the balcony of our condominium like moths to a flame. We arrange two chairs together, maybe put a light blanket on our knees, and sit side by side as the moon casts a silver path across the water.

During a full moon phase, everything seems to pause. The ocean glows. The waves shimmer like they've been lit from within. Even the breeze feels more poetic, like it knows it's part of something special. There's a romance that hangs in the air—not flashy or dramatic—but slow, still, and sure. It's in the quiet conversation, the laughter over a shared memory, the way her hand fits into mine without her needing to say a word.

That balcony becomes a front-row seat to something transcendent. It's a reminder that the best moments in life aren't always planned or posted. Sometimes they come wrapped in moonlight and carried on the sound of waves, reminding us why we chose each other in the first place. That's the kind of moonshine I'll choose every time. There's just one thing though. It's not the moon shining —it's the sun doing the shining.

The moon contains no properties that give it the ability to emanate its own light. All it's doing is reflecting the light from another source—the sun. The reason we see the light so clearly coming off the moon is because of its proximity to the sun and us. It appears luminous, even powerful, but it's a borrowed brilliance. That reflection can be breathtaking, even necessary on the darkest nights, but we often forget that the moon is not the source of light.

This is the danger of vocational moonshine. When we mistake the reflected light of our career for the core light of our purpose, we build our lives around something that was never meant to sustain our identity.

A role can *reflect* your purpose, but it can't *replace* it. The closer your role, title, or status gets to your identity, the brighter it may seem and the easier it becomes to confuse that borrowed glow with the real thing. But when circumstances shift—when retirement comes, or the business sells, or the title is handed to someone else—that light fades fast. And unless you've done the work of anchoring your identity to the source, you're left in the dark.

True vocational alignment begins when we stop orbiting the moon and turn back toward the sun. That's why I do the work I do. Because when the glow of the role fades, too many leaders are left disoriented, unsure of who they are without the title they once carried.

In my work with business owners and executives who are contemplating the close of their careers, I've discovered that they struggle with the same sense of loss of identity that I did when I lost my career. *Who am I if I'm not the ___?* is the overarching question in the mind and heart of a near-retirement executive. *Who am I if I'm not the owner of ___?* is the predominant question in the mind and heart of a business owner in the process of exiting or succession.

REFLECTIONS AND EXPRESSIONS

The truth is, we can never lose our identity. We take ourselves everywhere we go. We cannot escape ourselves.

When I present the moonshine principle to someone wrestling with this foundational question, I point out what I learned personally. In the metaphor, the person is the sun; the role of the business owner or executive is the moon. The role is a *reflection* of their identity. We are not defined by what we do. We are defined by who we are. What we do is the *expression*—what other people experience of who we are. Let me explain with a couple of examples.

My wife watches our three-year-old grandson on Wednesdays. When I'm home working, I have been known to take a break and get down on the floor and play with him. Our imaginary garage and police car chasing across the living room floor is Wesley's experience of who I am. I value my relationship with Wesley, so I express that by taking the time to enter his imaginary world and spending time with him. Incidentally, I am experiencing who Wesley is at the same time. We are experiencing each other's identity.

Here's another example. I am on the rotation of several worship teams at my local church. My role is to play the piano or keyboard. We normally rehearse on Thursday evenings before the Sunday we are scheduled to serve. Then on Sunday, we arrive at 7:00 in the morning and run through the order once or twice before the three services that morning. Now, that position is not what defines who I am. It's an expression of who I am. I know how to play piano. I value worship. I value music. When I play the piano, that is other people's experience of who I am.

These are just two examples of dozens I could share. The truth is, we have a plethora of moons circulating around our identity, like planets revolving around the sun. I have a marriage moon; each of my kids and their spouses represent four more moons. The four grandkids are four more moons. My role as coach and consultant is another moon. I'm a neighbor to those who live near me, which is another moon. And on and on it goes. These are all expressions of who I am.

The moonshine is important to grab hold of when talking about vocational alignment. So many of us hang on too long to a vocation under the mistaken assumption that it's the definition of who we are at the core of our being. We think if we retire or step down, we will abandon who we are, that we will lose our essence. So, we hang on too long and eventually do damage to the organization or relationships that are impacted.

When we finally grasp that our identity is far more expansive than our profession or title, a remarkable shift happens. We're no longer trapped in the illusion that our value is tied solely to what we do. That clarity opens the door to explore other vocational "moons" that may have been orbiting in the background all along—mentoring, caregiving, volunteering, creating, teaching, and leading in new ways.

This broader view of vocation allows us to realign our lives to fit the season we're actually in, not the one we've outgrown. We stop white-knuckling roles we've outlived, and we start moving with the current of purpose, not against it.

The fear of losing our identity fades because we realize we're not losing ourselves; instead, we're recovering ourselves. In fact, the more vocationally aligned we become, the more clearly our true identity begins to shine. Alignment creates freedom. And freedom makes it far more natural to live as the person we were uniquely designed to be. No posturing. No more feeling like we have to prove ourselves. Just presence, purpose, and peace.

> *Freedom makes it far more natural to live as the person we were uniquely designed to be.*

SIGNS YOU'RE LIVING UNDER MOONSHINE

Again, there's no way you can lose your identity, and what you do is a reflection of who you are. But it's possible to still be operating under the influence of moonshine. Here are thoughts to consider along this line.

There's a subtle but deeply unsettling feeling that creeps in when your sense of self is too tightly fused with your career. It's not always dramatic. Sometimes it shows up in quiet moments—like when a weekend feels aimless, or a vacation feels unnerving because you're not "producing" anything. This is often the first sign of vocational misalignment. When the work stops, even briefly, you begin to feel irrelevant. Not because you are, but because you've come to believe your relevance is tied to your output.

Emotionally, this creates tension that's hard to name. You might feel anxious when things slow down. You might notice you're unusually resistant to change—not because the change is bad, but because it threatens the identity you've constructed through your role. Even minor shifts in your professional responsibilities can create disproportionate discomfort because they disrupt the orbit of the one "moon" you've bet everything on.

This emotional undercurrent drives behavior that looks like commitment on the outside but is often avoidance on the inside. You say yes to every opportunity, every meeting, every new project—not out of alignment with purpose, but out of fear of what might surface if you stop. Busyness becomes a buffer. Activity becomes a substitute for clarity. And reflection feels threatening because it might force you to confront the truth: You've built your identity around a role that was never meant to define you.

Socially, the symptoms are just as clear. You find it hard to connect outside of work-related conversations. Small talk feels empty. Deep relationships feel distant. You show up in rooms where your job title once carried weight, and when it's no longer relevant, you don't know what to say. The discomfort isn't about others, it's about not knowing who you are when stripped of the label.

You'll often hear it in the phrases people use when they're trapped in the moonshine mindset. Perhaps you've uttered them yourself. "I don't know who I am without this." "I'm too valuable to walk away." "What would I even do all day?" These statements reveal confusion. They reveal fear—fear of invisibility, fear of wasting potential, fear of becoming ordinary after a life of being needed.

But the problem isn't that you're no longer useful. No, it's that your definition of usefulness has never matured beyond your career. And until that definition expands, you'll stay stuck, although active. Respected perhaps, but vocationally misaligned and emotionally adrift.

Does that describe you? Do you feel like you are vocationally misaligned and in need of a way to break free of the chains that bind you to your vocation? Before you can realign your vocation, you have to untangle your identity from your role. That starts with honest reflection.

VOCATIONAL SOBRIETY

Before we can realign our vocation, we have to untangle our identity from our role. That starts with honest reflection. Too often, our sense of self becomes so intertwined with what we do that we forget who we are beneath the job title, the business card, or the responsibilities we carry.

Too often, our sense of self becomes so intertwined with what we do that we forget who we are beneath the job title, the business card, or the responsibilities we carry.

This process of honest reflection is what I call *vocational sobriety*. It's the moment you wake up from the intoxication of your professional significance and begin seeing your life with clear eyes. Sobriety doesn't mean you discard everything you've done. Instead, you stop using your career as a substance to mask your deeper questions: Who am I really? What matters now? Where should my best energy go this season? Achievements, titles, and influence may have once fueled you—and served you—but they can't sustain you forever.

> *Achievements, titles, and influence may have once fueled you—and served you—but they can't sustain you forever.*

Vocational sobriety is the discipline of returning to "center." It's where you begin noticing the subtle misalignments, the orbit drift, the roles you're clinging to out of habit or fear rather than purpose. It takes courage to sit in that space without rushing to fill the silence with another job or another project. But it's in that sober stillness that you begin to see clearly again. And from there, you can begin to live—not by default, but by design.

The following exercises are designed to interrupt that drift. They'll help parts of you surface that may have been overshadowed by your professional identity. They'll begin clarifying what's still true even if your current role changes or disappears. Don't rush through them. Let your answers surprise you.

Exercise 1: Who Are You Without Your Work?

This might be harder than it sounds, and that's the point. If everything you write comes back to your career, it's a sign that your identity has collapsed into your output. Push past the default. Think about:

- Core values that define your character
- Life experiences that shaped you
- Roles you play outside work (e.g., spouse, friend, coach, servant)
- Things that bring you joy, curiosity, or peace
- Skills or traits you've developed that aren't tied to your job

Examples:

1. I'm a lifelong learner.
2. I value loyalty and truth.
3. I love being a grandfather.
4. I'm curious about how people make decisions.
5. I enjoy meaningful one-on-one conversations.
6. I find peace near the ocean.
7. I'm someone who shows up when others are hurting.
8. I love reading biographies.
9. I pay close attention to what people *don't* say.
10. I'm drawn to spiritual questions.

Write down ten things about yourself that have nothing to do with your job title, business, or professional achievements.

1. _____

2. _____

3. _____

4. _____

5. _____

6. _____

7. _____

8. _____

9. _____

10. _____

Now ask yourself:

- How many of those things are getting your time, energy, and attention right now?
- Which ones have been buried under your professional identity?

Exercise 2: If It All Ended Tomorrow

Answer this question honestly: If your career, business, or main professional identity ended tomorrow, what part of you would still be standing?

Answer here:

_____

_____

_____

_____

Use the space below to explore:

- What remains?
- What would feel like a loss?
- What would feel like relief?
- Who would you still be to the people who matter most?
- Where would your purpose reemerge?

This is not about planning your next gig. It's about testing the strength of your identity foundation. The goal is to determine whether your sense of self is rooted in who you are or just in what you've built.

Journal Prompt (optional):

- If the role I'm known for disappeared tomorrow, I would still be ...
- I would miss ...
- I would rediscover ...
- I would be free to explore ...
- I would need to grieve ...
- I would begin ...

THE ROLE OF VALUES

Remember the example of my grandson Wesley? The reason I took time out of my day to play in his world was driven by an inner value of influencing his life positively. I value relational richness as it relates to Wesley's life (and all of my grandkids, for that matter). It's this value that is so powerful. Values have such a strong place in vocational alignment that I want to devote a section just to them.

When the roles we've held start to shift—whether as a result of a season we're experiencing or a new stage of life we've entered—the first question that usually surfaces is about what we do now. But that's not the question that leads to clarity. The better question is about what we value.

Values are the foundation beneath every meaningful decision. They are the collective internal compass that remains steady even when external structures change. Knowing what you truly value gives you the ability to assess new opportunities, let go of old attachments, and realign your vocational energy with what actually matters to you—not just what's familiar.

Without clearly defined values, we tend to drift. We say yes to things because we always have. We hold on to roles that no longer fit because we don't know what else might give us meaning. This is what it means to live life by default. Our decisions are subject to how we are feeling, our mood, or what we think others think we should do. But when our values are clear, we are no longer guessing.

You can look at a commitment or a role and ask if it reflects who you are and what you stand for. That single question can prevent years of misalignment. Now this is what it means to be living by design. Our decisions are strategic and meaningful. They are mood proof.

Values act like guardrails during vocational transitions. They won't tell you the exact path, but they'll keep you from veering too far off course. If you value creativity, then any future vocation—paid or unpaid—needs space for that to thrive. If you value time with family, then a high-demand position that drains you might need to be reconsidered. Values don't just inform what you do, they also define the conditions in which you'll thrive doing it.

And perhaps most importantly, knowing your values permits you to evolve. Just because you once valued status or competition or financial growth doesn't mean those things still belong at the center. Vocational realignment doesn't mean you merely change directions; you are returning to what really matters. The clearer you are about your values, the more natural it becomes to navigate that return with purpose and peace.

REDISCOVERING YOUR VALUES

Rediscovering your personal values is one of the most critical steps in breaking free from vocational moonshine. Rick writes about values and virtues in chapter 2, and why they are important—both to develop as a person and to recognize them in others. When your work has long defined you, it's easy to forget what actually drives you, what makes your decisions feel right, what brings meaning to your days, and what keeps you grounded when everything else is shifting. Without that internal clarity, you can tend to chase familiar roles, replicate old patterns, or make decisions based on pressure instead of purpose.

Many people confuse values with ideals. They list what they think *should* be important: things that sound good on paper or align with social expectations. But rediscovering your *actual* values means identifying what already shows up in your life when no one's watching. What I'm talking about is the work of noticing where your time, energy, and attention naturally go when you're not trying to impress anyone.

This kind of self-honesty doesn't happen by accident. It requires intentional reflection and practical structure. The good news is you already have the answers. They're hidden in your habits, your preferences, your frustrations, and your patterns of joy. The goal isn't to create values you admire, it's to uncover the values you live by. Once you do, everything from vocational decisions to daily priorities begins to fall into place with greater ease and alignment.

In my early work with clients, I used a common values clarification exercise. I handed them a list of fifty value words and asked them to narrow it down to twenty, then ten, and eventually five. The idea was that those final five would represent their core values. It was simple, clean, and made for a nice coaching moment. But as time went on, I began to see its limitations. More often than not, people chose values they *wanted* to be true, not the ones they were actually living out. It became more of an exercise in aspiration than alignment.

Then I came across a different approach that completely shifted how I help people to uncover what truly matters. Instead of choosing from a list of nice-sounding words, this process invites you to observe your actual life, your time, your money, your attention, your patterns, and then extract your values from what's already there. It's about identifying what's real, not what's ideal.

The exercise below is based on that method. It's practical, grounded, and honest. And it's incredibly helpful if you're trying to break free from vocational moonshine. The more clearly you understand what you truly value, the easier it becomes to evaluate whether your current roles and responsibilities align with the season you're in. This is how you begin the realignment process—not by guessing or copying someone else's path, but by starting with who you already are.

Rediscovering Your Values

Your daily schedule and lifestyle choices reveal recurring themes that point to your true priorities—not aspirational ideas but real-world evidence. Clues are everywhere, so try the following exercise. Take your time writing your answers.

Purchases and Possessions

Look at your Amazon order history from the past two years to see what you like to buy.

Have a look in your shed or storage room to see what you hang onto.

Walk around your house to see what you put on display.

What would you keep if you could only take ten things from your home?

Free Time and Energy

Imagine it's a Saturday and you have four hours to yourself. No one has given you a to-do list, and the house is clean. What will you do?

What do you always look forward to?

What could you do or talk about for two hours and still feel excited about after?

When in your life have you felt most proud?

Organization and Habits

What do you love to keep organized? This could be a schedule or things you own.

What are the three organizational apps you use the most on your phone?

Thought Patterns and Reflections

You're in a chair on a back porch for two hours. What do you think about?

When you think of the future, what have you invested time in making happen?

Learning and Growth

What are your favorite books about?

What do you spend time learning about?

What do you help people with the most?

Look for repeated themes, phrases, or categories in your answers. Circle any words or ideas that show up in multiple answers. These patterns are your values rising to the surface. Aim to narrow your list down to 5–7 core values that resonate deeply and describe who you are, not who you wish you were.

Next, I want us to explore how to take those values and use them as a filter for realigning your vocational decisions and life direction.

USING YOUR VALUES FOR
VOCATIONAL ALIGNMENT

Now that you've clarified your true values—not the aspirational ones, but the ones that show up in your actual life—you're holding a powerful tool for realignment. These are signals. They tell you where your energy flows most naturally. They reveal what matters deeply, what motivates you, and what will continue to matter even after a title is gone or a role changes. But before we talk about how to use your values as a filter for vocational alignment, I want to point out how misalignment happens.

Vocational misalignment rarely comes from a lack of opportunity—it comes from overload. Most people aren't stuck because nothing is available to them; they're stuck because too much is available. Too many roles, too many obligations, too many "moons" pulling at their time, energy, and attention. The result is a life filled with activity but void of clarity. That's where values come in. When clearly identified, their values act like a filter, cutting through the clutter and helping them see which roles are worth keeping, which need to shift, and which have simply run their course.

The truth is, many of the moons currently orbiting around us are never a reflection of who we are—they just made sense at the time. Maybe they offered a sense of significance, helped bridge a transition, or kept the peace with someone else's expectations. But left unchecked, those same roles begin to pull us off course. We stay involved out of habit, fear, or obligation—even when we know, deep down, that they no longer align with what we value most. These aren't always bad things; they're just no longer the *right* things. And over time, they drain more than they give.

You may have heard that good is the enemy of great. Most of us don't start a moon with the intention of doing harm. We start a moon because it's good. But not all good moons are aligned moons.

Rediscovering your values gives you a way out of that fog. It brings clarity. It gives you language for what's no longer working and a compass for what should come next. And you are re-aligning with what matters most in this season or stage of your life.

Here's how you begin to use your values as a filter for re-alignment:

1. Run Every Role Through the Values Filter

List your current vocational commitments—paid and unpaid. For each one, ask:

- Does this align with one or more of my top values?
- Does it drain me or energize me?
- Am I doing it out of obligation, ego, or genuine alignment?

Vocational Commitment: _____

Vocational Commitment: _____

Vocational Commitment: _____

Vocational Commitment: _____

Vocational Commitment: _____

Vocational Commitment: _____

Vocational Commitment: _____

If a role doesn't connect to any of your values, and it consistently drains you, it's a candidate for release or restructuring.

2. Check for Value-Vocation Gaps

Sometimes a role aligns in theory but not in practice. Maybe you value creativity, but your leadership role has become nothing but operations and management. Or maybe you value relationships, but you're buried in solo tasks. Don't rush to abandon the role—consider whether it can be realigned to better reflect your values.

Ask:

- Can this role evolve to honor what I value more?
- Am I the one keeping it misaligned by avoiding necessary change?

3. Spot the Impostors

There are roles we say yes to because they look like they match our values, but in reality, they're fueled by image management or fear. For example, serving on a board may seem aligned with your value of contribution, but if you're only doing it for visibility or status, you'll eventually feel the misalignment. Your values help you tell the difference between real alignment and vocational moonshine.

4. Design Your Next Vocational Chapter Intentionally

Instead of jumping into the next role that presents itself, take your top 5–7 values and reverse-engineer your next season of contribution.

Ask:

- What would it look like to give my best energy to these values in this stage of life?

- What roles, projects, or opportunities would allow me to live these values consistently?
- What does this season *require* of me, and what can I release?

Values give structure to your freedom. They prevent you from drifting into new forms of busyness that look good on the outside but leave you hollow on the inside.

5. Use Your Values to Set Boundaries and Pace

Once you know what's most important, you're free to say no without guilt. You say yes or no, and you know why you're saying it. You don't owe anyone a packed schedule. You were designed to live a life that reflects what matters. Your values are the permission slip you've been waiting for to slow down, pivot, reimagine, and let go.

I'm proposing a way of life that isn't about making one big change. Instead, think of it as making aligned choices consistently over time. When your values lead, your life takes on a different rhythm. You stop chasing validation and start contributing from a place of freedom. That's what vocational alignment looks like—not perfection, just clarity and congruence.

VOCATIONAL ALIGNMENT AND YOUR LEGACY

At the time of writing this, my siblings and I are in Ohio helping Dad pack up all the stuff in his condominium so he can sell it and move from where we were all raised to his new home in Florida. As we were packing up his photos, memorabilia, files, knick-knacks, and books (oh, the books—Dad was a lover of books), something occurred to my siblings and me. We never really said anything, but we would look at each other, and we each knew it. What was going to storage was eventually going in the trash.

But we kept with the program Dad wanted. We boxed up all the stuff regardless.

The interesting thing that came to my mind was this: Each item held a place in his life for a time. Now they were destined for disposal by way of a temporary stay in storage. What lasts is the people moving in and out of the condo, packing boxes, and taking them to the garage. Dad's legacy is not a book or a photo or a favorite object on a shelf. His legacy is in the people he influenced while we did life together.

Your Legacy

So, let's talk about the legacy you're leaving right now. Even if you're not thinking about it, you're leaving it by the way you express your values and how you live. Rick goes into great detail about legacies in chapter 8, including how to write a legacy letter that will leave a lasting impression.

Legacy, in the context of vocational alignment, isn't about what we leave behind someday, but how we live right now. It's the cumulative effect of how we show up, what we value, and where we choose to invest our limited time, energy, and attention. When our roles reflect our true identity and not just our career titles, we begin shaping a legacy intentionally and strategically—living by design, not by default. We shape a legacy that's consistent, meaningful, and lasting—one that doesn't depend on status, but on alignment.

Too often, legacy is thought of as the sum of our professional achievements or the final sentence written in our obituary; something built from titles, bank accounts, or buildings with our name on the wall. But real legacy isn't established in retrospect; it's shaped in real time by the decisions we make every day about where we give our mental and physical investment. That's why vocational alignment matters so much.

Legacy is not built by accident. It is the natural result of living in alignment with your deepest values over time. It's the impression others carry after experiencing the truest version of you. And if you've spent your career operating under the influence of vocational moonshine—mistaking your role for your identity—then you know how easy it is to confuse impact with image.

When we live vocationally misaligned, we may accomplish a great deal, but we risk building a legacy that's disconnected from who we really are. We spend decades climbing ladders, only to find they were leaning against the wrong wall. We stay too long in roles we've outgrown. We chase results but lose sight of relationships. We pour ourselves into the work but forget what that work was supposed to serve.

Vocational alignment brings us back to our center. It invites us to examine our current season and stage of life and ask if this is the right use of *us* right now. It's not about abandoning everything that came before. Rather, it's about stewarding what remains. Alignment honors both the past and the future. It acknowledges the importance of what we've done but refuses to let that define what comes next. That's the turning point. That's where legacy gets real.

I told the story of losing my business. At that moment, the phone call, the collapse, the grief were more than merely the loss of a company. They were a disruption to the identity I'd built over decades. For a time, I equated my role with my worth as a human being. And when the role disappeared, it felt like my purpose had too. That's the emotional cost of vocational misalignment. But in the clarity that followed, I discovered something more enduring: My identity didn't die with my title. It was still intact, waiting to be rediscovered and redirected. That discovery is the foundation of a meaningful legacy.

A legacy of vocational alignment is not about how long you held a role. Legacy is in how clearly your values showed up in what you did. For me, it's found in the grandson who remembers me crawling on the floor to play, not because it is productive, but because it matters. It's in those moments at a keyboard on Sunday mornings, where my love of worship expresses itself through music—not to prove anything, but because it flows naturally from who I am. These aren't side stories. They're the *real* story. They're the moons that reflect my identity with clarity and consistency. Every aligned choice I make reinforces that legacy.

Think again about vocational sobriety, the clear-eyed moment where you stop using work to prop up your identity and begin asking better questions. That moment, sobering as it may be, is where legacy truly begins. Because legacy doesn't come from volume. Legacy comes from integrity. It's the accumulation of aligned decisions, intentional pauses, reevaluated commitments, and values-driven pivots. In that way, your legacy isn't something you have to start building later. You're building it now.

When you say no to roles that no longer fit, you're building a legacy on purpose. When you reassign time to what matters in this season, you're building a legacy on purpose. When you refuse to chase what's shiny and instead invest in what's meaningful, you're building a legacy on purpose. When you acknowledge that a former moon no longer reflects your light and you let it go with grace, you're building a legacy on purpose.

And this is critical: Legacy is not measured in permanence. It's measured in *presence*. Are you fully present with what matters? Are you aligned in this stage of life? Do your values translate into how you show up today?

That's the gift of vocational alignment. It allows your legacy to reflect your identity—not your résumé. It allows you to be remembered for who you were, not just what you did.

So, when you think about the impact you want to have—when you think about how your children, grandchildren, community, or peers will experience your life—ask yourself:

- Am I giving my best time and energy to what I value most?
- Am I holding onto moons that no longer reflect who I am?
- Have I mistaken vocational moonshine for true alignment?
- What adjustments, small or significant, will allow my life to reflect the legacy I want to leave?

The beautiful truth is that legacy is fluid. It evolves as we evolve. And you are not too late to realign. This may be the most important time to do so. You don't need a stage to leave a legacy, just congruence. You don't need to be impressive, just intentional. You don't need to control the outcome; simply live in alignment with who you truly are. And when you do, you'll discover something profound: Your legacy won't be what people remember after you're gone. It'll be what they *experience* while you're still here.

From Moonshine to Sunlight

Vocational alignment isn't a one-time decision. It's a lived process—revisited, refined, and recalibrated as we move through life's shifting stages. If you've made it this far, you've likely seen parts of your own story mirrored in these pages. You've recognized the pull of moonshine, the intoxicating glow of a role or title that once felt like everything. You've felt the ache of misalignment when the effort no longer yielded the same meaning. And you've probably wrestled with the core question that haunts many in transition: Who am I now?

That question haunted me too.

In the opening story of this chapter, I shared the day I lost my role as CEO of our family business that had stood for over four decades, serving churches and building spaces for worship across the country. It wasn't just the loss of a job. It was the unraveling of an identity I didn't even realize I had overattached to. For years, I had been the operator, strategist, and leader. My calendar reflected it. My conversations confirmed it. And my sense of worth was deeply entangled with it. So, when that final phone call came—the one that sealed the fate of the company—I lost more than a paycheck. I lost a part of myself. Or at least, I thought I did.

What I've discovered since that day is something I now carry into every coaching conversation, every retreat, every quiet session with someone standing at their own vocational crossroads: Your role is not your identity. It can reflect who you are, but it cannot *define* who you are. That distinction is the heartbeat of the moonshine principle.

Your role is not your identity.

The moonshine principle taught us that just like the moon doesn't produce light but reflects it, our roles—whether impressive or invisible—simply reflect something deeper. And when the reflection fades, the source remains. If we've done the work of anchoring our lives to the source—our values, our purpose, our truest identity—we don't fall apart when a chapter ends. We realign. We adjust the orbit. We find the next moon that matches the light we carry.

That's what vocational alignment is all about. It's the practice of giving your time, energy, and attention to what truly matters *now*, not what mattered in the last season or what others expect in this one.

For some people, alignment means stepping into something new. For others, it means stepping away from something that no longer fits. And for most, it means making subtle, consistent shifts in how we spend our days, how we show up in relationships, and how we define success moving forward.

The exercises I shared with you are not just empty space fillers. I've provided them to help you reclaim yourself. By asking who you are without your work, by considering what remains if your current title disappeared, you've begun the process of vocational sobriety. You've started to clear the fog that moonshine creates and are starting to see yourself—perhaps for the first time in a long time—with unfiltered clarity.

And then there are values. If moonshine is the illusion, your values are the lenses that keep you honest. They don't lie. They don't shift with market trends or organizational changes. Your true values—identified not by what you hope to be but by how you naturally live—become your north star. When life feels loud, when new roles present themselves, or when the fear of irrelevance creeps in, your values help you remember what matters. They help you say no with confidence. They help you say yes without guilt.

But here's the part that too many people miss. Values guide us in two directions: forward but also back. Back to ourselves. Back to the person we were before the title, before the expectations, before the pace swallowed up the purpose. Vocational realignment is often less about reinvention and more about return. A return to what brings joy. A return to the kind of presence that makes our relationships richer. A return to meaningful contribution that isn't measured by metrics but by impact.

Let's revisit the metaphor of the sun and moon one last time. Your identity is the sun. It has its own light, its own gravity, its own consistency. It doesn't go away when clouds pass. It doesn't depend on applause to shine. Your vocational moons are simply reflections of that deeper source. And when one moon fades, another can emerge. Some will orbit closer in certain seasons. Others will drift out or disappear. But you remain. Bright. Constant. Anchored.

This perspective is what sets the stage for legacy. When we live vocationally aligned, we stop striving to *be* impressive and start working to *leave* an impression on our families, our communities, and the people we quietly serve through presence and integrity. Legacy isn't built through achievement alone. It's built through alignment—when who we are, what we do, and what we value all move in the same direction.

If you find yourself at a crossroads—retiring, selling a business, changing careers, or simply sensing the misalignment of staying too long in a role you've outgrown—consider this your permission to pause. Don't race toward the next thing just to fill the void. Take time to listen, to observe, to realign. Let your values lead. Let your purpose—not your past performance—inform you of your next step.

The moment I lost my role, I thought I had lost myself. What I now know is that I was actually getting reintroduced to myself. That closing wasn't an ending but a recalibration. It forced me to stop orbiting a moon that had run its course and turn back toward the source of who I am. That experience didn't diminish my identity. Quite the contrary, it clarified it.

So, if you're facing your own vocational shift, don't fear it. Lean into it. Revisit your values. Audit your commitments. Pay attention to what energizes you. Get curious about the roles you've assumed and the ones you've been avoiding. And most of all, remember this: You were never the moon. You've always been the sun.

Let your next quarter of life reflect that. Live aligned.

CHAPTER 5

FINANCIALLY FREE

By Kent Kuhlmann

THE FOURTH QUARTER:
HOW TO LIVE WELL AND WORRY LESS

I am a firm believer in seeking counsel. I've done it my entire life. I'll be the first to admit that I don't know everything—not even close! So, once again, I sought wise counsel for this chapter, which brings me to my friend Kent.

Over the course of two decades, we have talked about money, the strategy of investing for growth, and the protection of assets. Our discussions seldom end with investing, but rather, the pain people go through with life events such as divorce, death, loss of principle, and a lack of planning, and how Kent can help people recover. Kent has a heart for people in their fourth quarter, and I love that about him. He cares!

As you process through this chapter, I encourage you to look through an imaginary lens that allows you to see where you *are* with finances and planning versus where you would like to be. There's a difference between the two. I did this in my early twenties because my parents struggled daily with their finances and I didn't want my future to look the same. Without going into great detail, I can sum it up by saying we were the recipients of the generosity of a family that took me (and not my brother) in for over one year, while my brother and I were in high school, to ease the financial burden on my parents. I looked through that lens and deliberately made changes early in life to ensure I would be financially free one day and generous with others. So, I encourage you to look through that lens regardless of your fourth-quarter investments and strategy, and make changes as needed. It's not too late. It's only too late if you don't react!

————

The later chapters of life offer a chance for clarity, simplicity, and intentional living. Health and purpose take priority, and money management—when planned with wisdom—becomes the fuel for a fulfilling journey rather than the destination.

After more than three decades advising individuals and families, I've learned that most people were never taught how to manage their finances effectively. They navigate rising costs, complex retirement rules, and fears of running out of money, often without a clear roadmap. Some oversave yet remain anxious. Others delay planning and hope for the best.

But the truth is this: the outcomes of your fourth quarter will be shaped more by your decisions than by your circumstances. Contentment, not accumulation, is the mark of real wealth.

Let's explore the five hallmarks of a strong, purpose-driven final quarter. This is your opportunity to align your finances with your values and live the life you were meant to enjoy.

#1: SIMPLIFY AND PROTECT YOUR ESTATE

One of the most meaningful gifts you can leave your loved ones is clarity. A well-organized estate plan minimizes confusion, reduces stress, and preserves relationships after you're gone.

Start with the basics: a will, a trust, and powers of attorney (POA) for both healthcare and finances. These documents ensure your wishes are honored, and they allow trusted individuals to act on your behalf if you're unable to. Without them, courts may decide who manages your affairs or receives your assets, creating delays and potential conflict. This is especially important with today's privacy laws—your family may be locked out of decision-making without proper authorization.

Review your documents regularly. Life changes—marriages, moves, new grandchildren, losses—all require updates to your plan. Equally important is to ensure your named beneficiaries on retirement accounts and insurance policies are current.

Consider a digital or physical estate organizer that includes all key contacts, account information, policy details, and legal documents. This isn't just for your attorney—it's also for the family member who will be standing in your place during a challenging time. I've provided a list of resources for this at the end of the chapter.

Finally, life insurance still has a role to play, even later in life. It provides tax-free liquidity and can be a crucial bridge for surviving spouses, heirs, or charities. Obtaining a life insurance policy in the fourth quarter can be expensive, so if the premiums do not fit into your budget, then consider a burial policy to cover expenses upon your death. This, too, will ease the financial burden on your family.

Estate planning isn't about having wealth—it's about stewarding what you've been entrusted. Clean it up. Simplify it. Then communicate your plan to those who need to know. This is why collaborating with a financial advisor, trust attorney, and tax preparer enables you to plan well and gives your heirs a clear path to follow.

#2: SECURE YOUR INCOME STREAMS

A predictable income is the foundation of a confident retirement. The fourth quarter should not be marked by financial stress but by financial clarity.

> *The fourth quarter should not be marked by financial stress but by financial clarity.*

Start by identifying your guaranteed sources: social security, pensions, and any annuities. Know when benefits begin and understand the implications of starting early versus waiting. Delaying social security can increase your lifetime benefits significantly, but it must be weighed against your health, family history, and immediate needs.

If you're married, coordinate your benefits. Spousal strategies, especially when one partner has significantly higher earnings, can optimize long-term security. Don't guess; model out different scenarios or consult a retirement income specialist. Consider how much of your basic living expenses can be covered by these reliable sources. If there's a gap between what you need and what's guaranteed, you'll need to draw from investments or consider adding supplemental income sources.

Also, factor in taxes. Many people forget that a sizable portion of retirement income, especially from individual retirement accounts (IRAs) and 401(k)s, will go to taxes. Due to the nature of the tax code, certain income sources present advantages over others in tax efficiency. This is why it is a good idea to have Roth IRAs—retirement accounts like IRAs and 401 (k)—and also an after-tax investment account, as all three of these are taxed differently. A smart withdrawal strategy can help minimize what you pay Uncle Sam and keep more of your money working for you.

If you are charitably inclined and give regularly to causes, a good strategy to consider is a qualified charitable deduction (QCD). When you cross an age milestone, currently seventy-three, the government forces you to begin withdrawals from your retirement plans, even if you don't need them. Even if you do, and are using taxed dollars to make donations, consider transferring money directly from your retirement account to the charity via a QCD. This way, you never take receipt of the money, so you don't pay taxes on the distribution, and the charity doesn't either. It is a very efficient way to support charities you hold dear.

And don't overlook inflation. What costs $1 today may cost $1.25 or more in a decade. Build in growth from investments or cost-of-living adjustments where possible to maintain your lifestyle over time.

The goal isn't just income—it's income that's stable, tax-aware, and designed to last as long as you do.

#3: DETERMINE YOUR BUDGET AND OPTIMIZE INVESTMENTS

A strong retirement begins with a clear understanding of your spending. Call it a budget, a cash flow plan, a spending plan, or simply a "retirement lifestyle map"—the goal is to know what's coming in, what's going out, and how long your money will last. Track your expenses for six to twelve months before retirement. Identify your fixed needs—housing, insurance, food—and your wants—travel, entertainment, hobbies. Many retirees underestimate discretionary spending, especially early in retirement when they're more active.

Build a margin for unexpected costs. Health events, home repairs, and family emergencies are part of life. A financial cushion—6 to 12 months of liquid savings—adds peace of mind.

Now match your spending plan with your investment strategy. Your portfolio should support your income needs but also grow enough to outpace inflation and extend your assets across a potentially long retirement.

One helpful model that I use with my clients is the "bucket strategy."

- Bucket 1 holds cash or short-term bonds to cover 12–18 months of expenses.
- Bucket 2 includes moderate-risk investments for income over the next 3–5 years.
- Bucket 3 focuses on long-term growth—stocks or exchange-traded funds (ETFs) that are not needed for 5+ years.

This layered approach helps you avoid panic selling during market dips and allows each portion of your portfolio to do its job.

Finally, review fees, tax efficiency, and asset allocation regularly. Investment success in retirement isn't about chasing the highest returns, but rather sustainability, protection, and confidence.

#4: PLAN FOR LONG-TERM HEALTHCARE

Few topics in retirement planning are as emotionally and financially complex as long-term care yet failing to prepare can derail even the most carefully crafted retirement plan.

The odds are real. My professional experience tells me that about 70 percent of people over the age of sixty-five will need a form of long-term care. That care may come at home, in assisted living, or in a skilled nursing facility. And it's expensive, routinely $4,000 to $10,000 per month, depending on the level and location of care.

Traditional health insurance and Medicare do not cover extended care services. Without a plan, the burden often falls on spouses or adult children. Start by having honest conversations. What are your care preferences? Who will advocate for you? What level of independence is nonnegotiable?

Explore your options early. Long-term care insurance is one tool, though it can be costly and complex. Alternatives include hybrid life insurance policies with long-term care riders or setting aside designated assets as a "care reserve." This is all part of building a spending plan—AKA budget—so that you can fund these items for the future. Understand Medicaid rules in your state if you're planning for worst-case scenarios. And remember: the best plan is one communicated clearly to your loved ones.

Long-term care isn't just about aging—it's about protecting dignity, relationships, and the legacy you've worked hard to build.

#5: LIVE PURPOSEFULLY

Financial freedom is not an end in itself—it's a tool to live with deeper purpose and joy.

As retirement unfolds, it's common for people to discover that what they truly crave isn't just leisure—it's meaning. Purpose comes from relationships, contribution, and growth. It's built in family dinners, mentoring a young person, starting a small venture, or volunteering in the community.

Studies consistently show that retirees who remain active—mentally, physically, and socially—live longer, healthier, and happier lives. Purpose protects your mind and spirit.

Start with gratitude. Each morning, reflect on what's good. Gratitude realigns your perspective and invites joy into the present moment.

Don't let retirement become isolation. Be involved in a healthy community of people. Build routines that engage you. Pursue creativity. Join a group. Take a class. Travel with intention. Stay curious. And pass on your wisdom. Write letters. Record your stories. Share your faith. These are gifts more valuable than money.

In the end, your purpose isn't measured by accomplishments but by love, service, and how well you lived your values.

KEYS TO A FULFILLING FOURTH QUARTER

The final quarter of life is not the finish line; it's the culmination. With intention and preparation, it can be the most meaningful season of all.

Here are ten timeless principles to guide your journey:

1. **Know your numbers**—Track income and expenses. Review them often.

2. **Eliminate bad debt**, especially high-interest or toxic obligations.

3. **Diversify income**—Layer Social Security, pensions, investments, and part-time income wisely.

4. **Reassess housing**—Make sure it supports your lifestyle and health as you age.

5. **Maintain a written plan**—Revisit it each year. Adjust as needed.

6. **Stay engaged**—Purpose and community matter more than ever.

7. **Keep a cash buffer**—Prepare for the unexpected without panic.

8. **Work with a professional**—A second set of eyes prevents blind spots.

9. **Allow yourself enjoyment**—You've worked hard. Live with balance.

10. **Lead with purpose**—Money is the means. Life is the mission.

You don't need to be wealthy to be free, but you do need a plan. And more than anything, you need to believe that the best is still to come.

RESOURCES

There are three recommendations for your consideration.

First, a financial planning tool found at www.goodsensemovement.org. They offer a computer program to optimize your spending plan or budget, and, when used properly, offer daily, weekly, monthly, and yearly updated expenditures according to your plan. With the instant update on your expenditure, you can adjust as needed to reach your goals.

Secondly, Rick Craig's book *When It's Time®: End-of-Life Planning at Any Age; Make It Part of Your Legacy* is an excellent book covering thirteen chapters on end-of-life topics. With a better understanding of these topics, one can make plans with confidence, which become part of your legacy and a gift to your heirs.

Thirdly, Rick Craig's book titled *"When It's Time®: An End-of-Life Workbook for Pre-Planners and Survivors"* is an excellent resource for recording pertinent information that you would want to share with a trusted family member or friend. Being a workbook, it also teaches you how to plan for the thirteen topics discussed in his first book.

CHAPTER 6

SPIRITUALLY ANCHORED

By Pastor Rick Craig

I n my early twenties, I received an invitation that seemed ordinary at the time, but it changed the course of my life. A close friend asked if I would go with her to church. I had heard of the pastor and knew a little about the congregation, and I didn't feel any pressure to say yes. It was simply an invitation; one I could easily have declined. But something in me said yes, and that one decision opened the door to something far greater than I could have imagined.

I walked into that church curious, yet a little uncertain. I didn't realize that God was already at work in me, drawing me, and stirring up questions I couldn't quite wrap my mind around. What began as an occasional visit soon became regular practice, and before long I found myself not only attending services but also hungry to learn. Week by week, as Scripture was opened and explained, my heart began to change. I discovered a depth of truth I hadn't known, and I began to sense that God was not distant, but nearby.

Looking back, I am amazed at the impact of that one invitation. It was not a demand, not an argument, not an ultimatum. It was simply a hand extended and a door opened. Over the years, I have given that same invitation to others. Sometimes the response was a polite refusal. Other times, curiosity drew them in. But when someone said yes, their life was transformed. Invitation is the language of grace. It doesn't force; it welcomes. It doesn't push; it opens a way.

The Scriptures are full of stories shaped by invitation. One of the most striking comes from John 4:1–42, when Jesus met a Samaritan woman at Jacob's Well. She came burdened, both by her reputation and the daily task of drawing water. She expected routine and drudgery; instead, she encountered grace. Jesus crossed cultural lines to speak with her—a Jewish rabbi addressing a Samaritan woman in public. He began with a request for water yet turned the conversation toward something eternal. He spoke of "living water" that would quench her thirst forever.

What strikes me most is the way He did it. Jesus named the truth of her life—the pain, the broken relationships, the disappointments—yet did so without condemnation. He spoke truth wrapped in compassion, and that combination ignited hope. The woman left her water jar behind—the very symbol of her daily struggle—and ran to her village to share what had happened. She became an unlikely evangelist, not because she had mastered theology but because she had encountered the Messiah. Her life was anchored to Him in a single conversation.

I wonder how many lives turn on the hinge of invitation. An invitation to church. An invitation to coffee. An invitation to pray. Sometimes the door to eternity opens through the simplest knock. And so, I begin this chapter the way my own story began: with an invitation.

This is not an invitation to religion or ritual. It is not an invitation to add another obligation to your already full schedule. It is an invitation to explore what it means to be anchored spiritually. To ask you to consider what holds you steady when life shakes you, where you turn when storms rise, or what you are building your life upon.

My prayer is that as you read these words, you won't hear pressure but possibility. You won't feel condemnation but curiosity. You won't sense distance but nearness. Because being spiritually anchored is not a burden to carry; it's a gift to receive. It begins not with your striving but with God's drawing. It begins with a loving gesture and a heart willing to respond.

So, I invite you to travel with me through this chapter. Come as you are. Bring your questions. Bring your doubts. Bring your longings. The God who met a Samaritan woman at a well and who met me as a young man sitting in a church is the same God who longs to meet you. And His invitation still stands: "Come, all you who are thirsty, come to the waters" (Isaiah 55:1).

WHAT ARE YOU CALLING YOUR ANCHOR?

Every person anchors their life to something. Some will center their lives on building careers and chasing security in wealth, others with relationships, believing family or romance will always steady them. Others lean on education, knowledge, or philosophy, hoping intellect will chart their course. Many simply trust themselves—their own resilience or determination. Still others turn to spirituality in vague forms—energy, the beauty of nature, or a "higher power" that offers comfort but remains undefined.

Anchors matter because life is full of storms. When the winds rise, when loss or betrayal strikes, when illness or disappointment comes, your anchor will either hold or it won't. I've seen too many people build their lives on something that looked steady, only to discover in crisis that it could not bear the weight.

My own journey began with Scripture. In 1977, as a young man searching for meaning, I came to believe that the Bible was not just ancient literature but the inspired Word of God. That realization changed everything. Scripture became the plumb line against which I measured my thoughts, decisions, and desires. It gave me a compass, a standard, a voice that spoke louder than culture. Two years later, on September 13, 1979, I confessed Jesus Christ as Lord and surrendered my life to Him. That confession wasn't a ritual. It was a moment of anchoring, driving a stake deep into the ground of God's promises.

Romans 10:9 says it plainly: "If you declare with your mouth, 'Jesus is Lord,' and believe in your heart that God raised him from the dead, you will be saved." That verse became not just a line in a book but a doorway I walked through. The anchor I chose wasn't philosophy or willpower or even religion. It was Jesus Himself—His death, His resurrection, His Word that cannot fail.

Over the years, storms came. I buried loved ones, wrestled with doubt, walked through seasons of grief and confusion. But through it all, my anchor held. Not because I am strong, but because Christ is. Hebrews 6:19 describes it best: "We have this hope as an anchor for the soul, firm and secure." Hope in Christ is not wishful thinking; it is a living, breathing certainty that steadies us when everything else shakes.

Let me ask you directly: What are you calling your anchor? Maybe you've relied on hard work. Maybe your anchor has been people you trust. Maybe it's your bank account. Maybe it's been a cause or a dream. Those can all be good things, but they were never meant to be the ultimate thing. When elevated to that position, they can't hold.

Think about it this way: a ship's anchor doesn't rest on the waves. It sinks deep, latching onto bedrock hidden beneath the surface. That's what Christ offers—not a surface solution that drifts with tides, but a grip on the unchanging foundation of God's truth. Everything else is shifting sand.

I once counseled a man who had built his whole identity on his career. He was successful, admired, and wealthy. Then an economic downturn wiped out his business almost overnight. The loss was devastating, not just financially but also personally. "I don't know who I am anymore," he told me, "because I'm not the man who built this company." His anchor had been his work, and when it failed, he felt unmoored. In time, through prayer, study, and the encouragement of community, he began to discover a deeper anchor in Christ. But I'll never forget the despair in his voice when his first anchor gave way.

Here's the beauty: Christ never gives way. He is the same yesterday, today, and forever (Hebrews 13:8). He does not rust or corrode. He does not weaken with time. When you make Him your anchor, you can weather storms with peace. Not because storms vanish, but because your soul is secured to the Rock that cannot move.

So again, I pose the question: What are you calling your anchor? If your answer is anything other than Christ, I invite you to reconsider. Not as a demand, not as a judgment, but as an invitation—the same invitation I accepted in 1977, the same invitation the Samaritan woman accepted at the well—to anchor your soul in the One who knows you, loves you, and will hold you fast.

THE PLUMB LINE: STARTING STRAIGHT

Builders understand the importance of beginning their projects with straight lines, which culminate in a building that is aligned and strong. Before laying bricks, before raising walls, they pull out a simple yet vital tool: the plumb line. It consists of a string with a weight at the bottom, used to ensure straight, vertical alignment. Builders have relied on this tool for centuries because gravity, which pulls the weight down, cannot be cheated or altered. It always points to the true vertical. The principle is clear: If you want the building to stand tall and firm, you must begin by using a reliable, unchanging standard.

Life works much in the same way. Many people think a little compromise here, a slight detour there, won't matter. But small deviations at the start become gaping errors over time. What begins as a "small" dishonesty, an ignored conviction, or a neglected discipline eventually warps character and corrodes trust.

God gave His people a vivid picture of this in Amos 7 (found in the Old Testament, aka Hebrew Scriptures). The prophet Amos saw the Lord standing by a wall with a plumb line in His hand. God declared that He was measuring His people—not according to their own standards, nor by comparison with other nations, but by His own unchanging truth. The vision was sobering: Israel had drifted so far out of plumb that judgment was inevitable.

The plumb line is not a symbol of cruelty but of grace. God reveals His standard so that His people may see where they've strayed and turn back. Just as a wise builder corrects as soon as the plumb line shows a problem, so a wise believer welcomes God's correction. To resist is to risk collapse. To realign is to preserve strength.

Jesus picked up this same theme. He told of two builders, one who built on sand and one who built on rock. Both houses looked fine on sunny days. Both offered shelter when the skies were clear. But when the storm came—and storms always come—only the house on the rock remained because it was aligned with the truth of God's Word (Matthew 7:24–27).

I've seen this play out countless times in ministry. A couple once came to me in crisis. On the outside, their life looked picture-perfect: careers thriving, children succeeding, a lovely home. But when tragedy struck, the foundation cracked. Their faith had been built on social respectability rather than Scripture. They hadn't built prayer into their marriage. They hadn't secured themselves in God's Word. The result was collapse under pressure. By God's grace, they found their way back, but not without deep pain. The plumb line had revealed what storms made visible.

Another man I knew ignored warning after warning about his private choices. To everyone else, he seemed faithful and devoted. But behind the scenes, compromises mounted. What began small—justifying sins as "not so bad"—grew into strongholds that consumed him. When the truth finally became known, his life was in ruins. Again, the plumb line had been there all along, quietly hanging, silently declaring, but ignored.

The lesson is simple: better to realign early than to rebuild after collapse. That's why daily Scripture matters. It's why prayer matters. They keep us close to the plumb line, checking our hearts and measuring our choices against God's unchanging truth.

Culture will always shift its standards. What was scandalous a generation ago is applauded today. What was once honored can be mocked tomorrow. But God's Word does not move. It is the true and final plumb line. Isaiah 40:8 reminds us that "the grass withers and the flowers fall, but the word of our God endures forever."

I often tell people they don't measure the plumb line against their wall; they measure their wall against the plumb line. In other words, Scripture doesn't bend to fit our preferences; we must bend to fit Scripture. It is not arrogance to say so; it is humility— humility to acknowledge that left to ourselves, we build crookedly. Humility to accept that we need an external, unchanging standard to guide us.

Here is the good news: God's plumb line is not only law, but also love. He gives it not to shame us, but to steady us. Like a father teaching his child to walk straight, God offers His Word so that we may walk in safety, in wisdom, and in life.

So, I ask you, what are you using to measure your life? If it is culture, it will shift. If it is feelings, they will deceive. If it is success, it will fade. Only God's Word remains true, steady, and straight. Align to it now before the cracks spread. Adjust today and you will stand tomorrow.

HEALING FROM THE PAST

No journey into spiritual anchoring can move forward without addressing the weight so many of us carry from yesterday. Doctors Charity Byers and John Walker discussed this in great detail in chapter 1. We try to press ahead, but the chains of regret, betrayal, loss, and guilt keep tugging us backward. To be grounded in Christ means not only to be secured for the future but also to be healed from the past. And at the very center of that healing is forgiveness.

OFFERING FORGIVENESS

Forgiveness is one of the most difficult commands Jesus ever gave. It feels impossible, unfair even. The hurt we carry is real; the wounds are deep. To forgive can feel like excusing the harm. But forgiveness is not a denial of justice. It is releasing the weight of bitterness from your own soul.

Jesus said that "if you forgive other people when they sin against you, your heavenly Father will also forgive you. But if you do not forgive others their sins, your Father will not forgive your sins" (Matthew 6:14–15 ESV). Those are strong words, but they are life-giving ones. Forgiveness is not optional if we want freedom; it is the path to freedom itself.

I once carried a wound inflicted by someone who betrayed my trust in a way that cut to the core. Every instinct in me wanted to hold on to anger, to keep replaying the offense. For months, that bitterness poisoned my heart, robbing me of peace. One day in prayer, I sensed the Lord whisper: *You can keep carrying this, or you can hand it to Me.* With a broken heart, I prayed a prayer of release. Nothing about the other person changed. They never apologized, never admitted wrong. But something inside me shifted. I was free.

That's the paradox of forgiveness: it's less about setting the offender free and more about setting yourself free. Forgiveness is releasing them into God's hands, trusting Him to judge rightly. It doesn't always mean reconciliation, especially in cases of abuse. But it always means release—laying down the burden that is crushing your soul.

RECEIVING FORGIVENESS

There's another side to this. Many of us are chained not by what others have done to us but by what we ourselves have done. We replay our failures. We whisper to ourselves: *What if people find out?* Shame becomes a prison, and even though Christ has opened the door, we remain sitting inside.

Romans 8:1 is a verse I often come back to: "There is now no condemnation for those who are in Christ Jesus." Notice the word *now.* Not later, not once you've cleaned yourself up, but now. The moment you are in Christ, condemnation is gone. Psalm 103:12 says, "As far as the east is from the west, so far has he removed our transgressions from us." God is not dangling your past over your head. He has cast it away, nailed it to the cross, and declared it finished.

I counseled a man once who had come to faith but could not let go of his guilt. He wept as he confessed his sins, convinced he was beyond repair. I read Romans 8:1 to him again and again, waiting for the words "now" and "removed" to infuse his mind. Slowly, he began to grasp that forgiveness was not something he had to earn, but something already purchased by Christ. Watching shame break off him was like watching a prisoner walk out of a cell into sunlight for the first time.

If you are weighed down by guilt today, hear this: Christ's forgiveness is enough. Don't dishonor His sacrifice by insisting your sin is greater than His grace. Healing comes when you trust that the blood of Jesus covers even the darkest chapter of your past.

WALKING IN FORGIVENESS

Imagine arriving at the airport with three suitcases in tow, and your children are pulling their own bags. Each bag has four wheels to assist you in making it easier to travel. Now imagine that one bag's wheel falls off; you can still drag it, but it's more difficult. Now, imagine the other two bags have wheel problems, and to compound the issue, one of your children asks you to drag their bag too. Your time to the gate is now prolonged, and you can feel the pressure. Will you make it to the gate on time, or will you be late? With each dynamic, the simple movement forward is complicated until you get to the point where it is impossible, and you arrive late at your gate.

Forgiveness is like having all the wheels of your bags working rather than laboring through the journey. The bags still exist, but they are no longer the problem. Forgiveness is like this. You are not heavily burdened anymore. You are now free.

Jesus teaches that holding on to unforgiveness affects not only our relationships with others but also our relationship with God. When we refuse to forgive, we close off our hearts to the healing God wants to offer us. By contrast, forgiving others opens the door to freedom and allows God to work in our lives in new and transformative ways. Spiritual growth happens best when our relationship with God the Father, Jesus the Son, and the Holy Spirit is unhindered. Sin steals good things from you, such as your relationship with God. Unforgiveness has the same effect.

Forgiveness isn't a one-time act; it's a daily walk. Paul wrote "Bear with each other and forgive one another if any of you has a grievance against someone. Forgive as the Lord forgave you" (Colossians 3:13). Forgive as—that's the key. We forgive not out of our own strength but out of the forgiveness we've already received.

> *Forgiveness isn't a one-time act;*
> *it's a daily walk.*

This means forgiveness becomes a lifestyle. It means we practice releasing offenses quickly instead of nursing them. It means reminding ourselves daily that we are forgiven; therefore, we forgive.

SCARS AND HEALING

Forgiveness doesn't erase memory. Scars remain. But scars are not signs of defeat; they are reminders of healing. Jesus Himself rose from the grave with scars on His hands and side. They were no longer wounds, but testimonies of victory.

Your scars can be the same. What once was a source of shame can become a story of grace. What once defined your pain can now display God's power. Healing doesn't mean forgetting; it means remembering differently.

So, let me ask you what you are carrying from the past that needs healing. Is it bitterness toward someone who wronged you? Is it shame over something you did? Is it grief that still feels raw? Whatever it is, Christ invites you to lay it at His feet. Forgiveness doesn't erase the past, but it frees your future.

Forgiveness doesn't erase the past,
but it frees your future.

Being spiritually secure means you are no longer tossed about by the storms of yesterday. You are rooted in the mercy of God, secured in His grace. The past loses its power, and your soul begins to breathe again. But even after you've tasted the healing power of forgiveness, your journey doesn't stop there. Each day brings new choices, and with them, the danger of missing the mark.

MISSING THE MARK

The Greek word for sin, *hamartia*, literally means "to miss the mark." It's a term from archery —the arrow flies, but it doesn't strike the target. Sometimes it falls short. Other times it veers just slightly off. But either way, the result is the same: the target is missed.

This is powerful imagery for our spiritual lives. Sin is not only open rebellion against God; it is also straying. A small compromise here, a subtle shift there, and before we know it, we are far from where we intended to be. No one wakes up one morning and says, "I want to ruin my marriage," or "I want to shipwreck my faith." But daily choices, even tiny ones, accumulate. The further we go, the greater the distance from the mark.

I recently spoke with a man who is in the military and a competition shooter using long-range rifles. He told me that at 100 yards, being off by just a fraction of an inch barely matters. But at 500 yards or more, that same small misalignment causes the bullet to miss the target by several inches. His words stuck with me. In life, being "just a little off" might not seem catastrophic today, but given time, it can lead to disaster.

Paul warned Timothy about this very danger. He wrote, "Timothy, guard what has been entrusted to your care. Turn away from godless chatter and the opposing ideas of what is falsely called knowledge, which some have professed and in so doing have departed from the faith" (1 Timothy 6:20). The believers of Paul's day were being drawn away by false teaching that sounded intelligent, even enlightened, but it led them off course." John 8:34 tells us, "Jesus replied, 'Very truly I tell you, everyone who sins is a slave to sin.'" Missing the mark is not a harmless mistake— if left unchecked, it leads to bondage.

Our culture makes this even harder, as standards shift constantly. What was condemned a generation ago may be celebrated today. What was once honored can be mocked tomorrow. If our aim is guided by culture, we will never strike the true target. God's Word alone is the bullseye. It never moves, never drifts, and never changes with the winds of opinion.

> *If our aim is guided by culture,*
> *we will never strike the true target.*

Here's the good news: in Christ, course correction is always possible. Unlike the archer who can't retrieve a released arrow, we are offered grace. God gives us second chances, new beginnings. 1 John 1:9 declares, "If we confess our sins, he is faithful and just and will forgive us our sins and purify us from all unrighteousness."

I have seen people come back from years of wandering. A husband who slowly neglected his faith found himself distant from his wife and children, but when he repented, God began to rebuild his life. A woman who embraced cultural philosophies discovered the emptiness of them, and through Scripture, she found her way back to Christ. Their stories remind me that no matter how far the miss, the Father's arms remain open.

Here's what this means for us: We must check our aim daily. Are we aiming at God's truth or our own desires? Are we aligning with Scripture or with culture? Are we allowing small compromises to add up?

Missing the mark doesn't have to be the end of the story. God's grace invites us to realign, to recalibrate our sights, to fix our eyes once again on Jesus. He is both the plumb line and the bullseye, the measure and the target. Steadfast in Him, we can live with confidence that when the arrows of our lives fly, they will strike true.

HE DRAWS US

Every story of faith begins not with us seeking God, but with God seeking us. Left to ourselves, we drift. Our hearts may hunger for meaning, but we rarely know where to look. Jesus made this truth clear, saying, "No one can come to me unless the Father who sent me draws them, and I will raise them up at the last day" (John 6:44). Faith is not simply our idea; it is God's initiative. It is humbling to think that God pursues a relationship with us, and that if we respond, we can be made new. 2 Corinthians 5:17 tells us that "if anyone is in Christ, the new creation has come: The old has gone, the new is here!"

Looking back on my own life, I can see how the Lord was drawing me long before I said yes to Him. At the time, I wouldn't have described it that way. I felt a restlessness, an unsettled sense that something was missing. I tried to fill it with distractions through relationships, busyness, and chasing success. But underneath, the longing remained. That was God. He was stirring the questions I couldn't name, nudging me toward a deeper reality.

Maybe you can relate. Perhaps you've felt that tug in quiet moments—when the noise fades and you sense there must be more. Maybe it comes during a sunset that takes your breath away, or in the stillness of the night when your thoughts wander. That hunger for meaning, that ache for more is not random. It is the whisper of God drawing you.

Scripture is full of such moments. God drew Moses from the wilderness with a burning bush (Exodus 3:1–6). He drew Samuel in the quiet of the night with a voice calling his name. He drew Isaiah with a vision of His holiness (1 Samuel 3:1–10). And He draws you and me with circumstances, with people, and with questions that stir our souls (Isaiah 6:1–8).

That hunger for meaning, that ache for more is not random. It is the whisper of God drawing you.

One of the most humbling parts of being a pastor has been watching this drawing unfold in people's lives. I've sat with skeptics who came to church only to appease a spouse, yet found themselves moved to tears during worship. I've prayed with men who swore they'd never believe, only to confess that something beyond them was tugging at their hearts. That "something" is really Someone—the Spirit of God. And here is the beauty: God does not draw us to shame us, but to save us. He does not lure us into rules and rituals but into relationship. *His drawing is always an invitation—come closer, trust deeper, receive grace.*

If you sense that tug in your life, don't ignore it. Don't brush it off as emotion. That hunger is holy. That restlessness is divine. The Father is drawing you, and He longs to anchor your soul in Him.

CHOOSING YOUR SPIRITUAL COMMUNITY

Faith was never meant to be lived alone. From the beginning, God designed us to be in relationship. Before sin entered the world, before brokenness scarred creation, God said, "It is not good for the man to be alone. I will make a helper suitable for him" (Genesis 2:18). That truth goes deeper than marriage—it speaks to our very nature. We were created for community.

The early church understood this. Acts 2:42–47 paints a vivid picture of believers and how they lived by saying,

They devoted themselves to the apostles' teaching and to fellowship, to the breaking of bread and to prayer. Everyone was filled with awe at the many wonders and signs performed by the apostles. All the believers were together and had everything in common. They sold property and possessions to give to anyone who had need. Every day they continued to meet together in the temple courts. They broke bread in their homes and ate together with glad and sincere hearts, praising God and enjoying the favor of all the people. And the Lord added to their number daily those who were being saved.

Growth wasn't driven by clever strategies or marketing; it flowed naturally from authentic community.

When storms hit, community becomes the lifeline that keeps us connected. I experienced this in one of the most painful seasons of my life. Within eighteen months, I buried my brother, my wife, and my mother. The grief was suffocating. There were days I could hardly pray, hardly breathe. Yet it was my small group—my spiritual family—that carried me. They brought meals. They wept with me. They prayed when I couldn't find words. Sometimes they simply sat in silence, their presence a reminder that I was not alone.

That is what true spiritual community looks like. Not perfection. Not performance. Presence. A willingness to walk together through joy and sorrow, to bear each other's burdens, and to point one another back to Christ. Galatians 6:2 says it simply: "Bear one another's burdens, and so fulfill the law of Christ" (ESV).

Choosing your spiritual community matters. Not every group that calls itself "church" will ground you in Christ. Some may stray from the truth, focusing on entertainment or personal agendas. Others may be so rigid that grace is absent. A healthy community will always be marked by four things: devotion to God's Word, commitment to prayer, genuine fellowship, and a spirit of service.

Accountability isn't always comfortable,
but it is always life-giving.

Community also challenges us. Proverbs 27:17 says, "As iron sharpens iron, so one person sharpens another." Left alone, we may excuse our faults, but in community, loving brothers and sisters call us higher. They remind us of who we are in Christ when we forget. They nudge us back to the plumb line when we drift. Accountability isn't always comfortable, but it is always life-giving.

Let's be honest: sometimes community is messy. People are imperfect. Conflicts arise. Misunderstandings happen. But here's the truth—even the mess can be holy ground. Working through differences with grace, choosing forgiveness in relationships, practicing patience and humility—all of it shapes us to look more like Jesus. This is what chapter 2 is all about: identifying, understanding, and growing in the key virtues for living well.

Hebrews 10:24–25 urges us to "consider how we may spur one another on toward love and good deeds, not giving up meeting together, as some are in the habit of doing, but encouraging one another—and all the more as you see the Day approaching." In other words, don't isolate. Don't drift. Stay connected. Stay engaged. The relationships derived from within your community can hold you steady when the storms come.

So, ask yourself who your community is. Who are the people you pray with, worship with, grieve with, and celebrate with? If you don't have such a group, ask God to lead you to one. And if you do, cherish them. Lean in. Be present. Because when you choose your spiritual community wisely, you discover that the anchor is not just personal, but shared. And together, with Christ, you will weather any storm.

LIVING YOUR FAITH

Faith was never meant to be a private possession, tucked away like a family heirloom gathering dust in the attic. Real faith is lived out, visible in choices, relationships, and priorities. It's not about being flashy or self-righteous, but about letting the reality of Christ shape everyday life. James put it bluntly: "Faith by itself, if it is not accompanied by action, is dead" (James 2:17).

Living your faith begins with transformation. Romans 12:2 urges, "Do not conform to the pattern of this world, but be transformed by the renewing of your mind. Then you will be able to test and approve what God's will is—his good, pleasing and perfect will." The currents of this world shout constantly: chase success, protect yourself, define truth your own way. But a renewed mind resists those streams. Instead of being pressed into the mold of culture, allow Scripture to shape your thoughts and the Spirit to guide your steps.

This transformation shows up in ordinary choices. A man once told me that when he began following Christ, the first thing that changed wasn't his career or his finances—it was the way he treated his employees. He moved from being harsh and demanding to leading with compassion and fairness. His faith spilled over into his leadership, and people noticed. Another woman quietly gave away part of every paycheck, long before she had "extra." Her generosity didn't make headlines, but it blessed an untold number of lives. That's living faith—not abstract belief, but embodied obedience.

Living faith also means living under the authority of God's Word. 2 Timothy 3:16–17 reminds us that "all Scripture is breathed out by God and profitable for teaching, for reproof, for correction, and for training in righteousness, that the man of God may be complete, equipped for every good work" (ESV). This doesn't mean every decision comes with a neat verse attached, but it does mean we filter decisions through the lens of Scripture. We ask: "Does this decision honor Christ?" "Does this reflect His character?" and "Does this align with His truth?"

I've often encouraged believers to picture Scripture as a set of eyeglasses. Without them, life is blurry, distorted, subjective. With them, everything comes into focus. Living faith means you refuse to view the world through the media or convenience; instead, you see through the lens of God's truth.

Living your faith will inevitably invite challenges. Jesus never promised popularity. In fact, He warned that following Him would bring opposition. But He also promised His presence, saying, "Surely I am with you always, to the very end of the age" (Matthew 28:20). The courage to live differently doesn't come from our resolve but from trust in Jesus, built on a growing relationship with Him.

Living faith is contagious. I've known men and women whose quiet witness spoke louder than any sermon. Their coworkers respected them because they lived with integrity. Their families admired them because they practiced forgiveness. Their neighbors trusted them because they consistently showed kindness. They weren't perfect, but their lives pointed others to Jesus.

So, how do we live our faith in practical ways? We begin with daily practices of prayer, Scripture, and worship. We seek wise counsel when making decisions. We practice generosity, not because we have surplus but because we trust God to provide. We look for opportunities to share our story, not with arrogance but with humility. And we stay sensitive to the Spirit, allowing Him to nudge us toward repentance when we drift.

Living your faith doesn't mean adding more religious activities to your calendar. It means infusing every area of life with the presence of Christ. Work becomes worship. Family becomes ministry. Even struggles become testimonies.

STEADFAST PEOPLE LIVE STEADFAST LIVES.

Their faith is not just professed on Sunday but practiced on Monday. And when storms hit, their witness shines brightest. People notice not how loudly they preach but how steadily they stand.

So, ask yourself: What does living your faith look like in your home? In your workplace? In your neighborhood? The answer won't be identical for everyone, but the essence is the same: Christ in you, the hope of glory, expressed in the details of daily life.

And as we practice this kind of faith in the ordinary details of life, we also discover its power in the extraordinary—the moments of testing, the storms that threaten to undo us. That is where living by faith leads to living in victory.

LIVING IN VICTORY

When people hear the word *victory*, they often picture a life without struggle—smooth seas, endless sunshine, no setbacks. But victory in Christ doesn't mean the absence of storms; it means peace in the middle of them. It's not about avoiding battles but about walking through them with a strength not our own.

Victory in Christ doesn't mean the absence of storms; it means peace in the middle of them.

Paul captured this paradox beautifully in Romans 5:3–5: "We also glory in our sufferings, because we know that suffering produces perseverance; perseverance, character; and character, hope. And hope does not put us to shame, because God's love has been poured out into our hearts through the Holy Spirit, who has been given to us."

Victory isn't the absence of hardship; it's the presence of hope that hardship cannot crush.

Jesus Himself warned His disciples, "I have told you these things, so that in me you may have peace. In this world you will have trouble. But take heart! I have overcome the world" (John 16:33). Notice the certainty: you *will* have trouble. Yet also notice the promise: *I have overcome.* The storms are real, but so is His triumph. Living in victory means anchoring your soul—not to changing circumstances but to the unchanging Christ.

I once spoke with a woman battling cancer. The treatments were brutal, the prognosis uncertain, yet she radiated peace. When I asked how she managed it, she said, "My body is sick, but my spirit is well. No matter what happens, I win because either I'm healed here, or I'm healed in heaven." That's victory. Not denial of pain, but defiant hope in the face of it.

Victory also means power over temptation. Sin whispers, offering counterfeit comfort, but anchored believers learn to lean on the Spirit's strength. Ephesians 6 guides us to put on the "armor of God": the belt of truth, the breastplate of righteousness, the shield of faith, the helmet of salvation, the sword of the Spirit, and the shoes of the gospel of peace (Ephesians 6:13–17). These are not abstract images; they are daily realities. Each morning, we choose to fasten truth around us, to guard our hearts with righteousness, to hold up faith when doubt attacks, to wield Scripture against the lies. That is how we stand in victory, even when temptation presses hard.

Victory means confidence in God's love. Romans 8 swells with the declaration that nothing—not death, not life, not angels, not demons, not the present, not the future, not any power—can separate us from the love of God in Christ Jesus (vv. 38–39). When you know you are secure in that love, fear loses its grip.

A friend of mine had an encounter with his five-year-old son. My friend was sitting on his couch, working on his laptop computer. His son was talking to him, but my friend wasn't really paying attention, so he was giving him courtesy responses as if he was listening intently and engaged in the conversation. Like most five-year-olds, his son wanted to be heard, so he took action. He walked up to his dad, lifted the laptop off his lap, put it aside, then crawled onto his dad's lap. With one hand on his dad's chest, he looked him in the eyes and said, "Talk to me with your eyes!" Ouch! But the impact that single gesture and statement made changed everything in their relationship. Not that my friend ever considered his son anything less than a gift he treasured, but it did develop a connection that has lasted over the last twenty-one years since that exchange.

Our Father in heaven and our Lord, Jesus, want that same kind of connection. That is why Yahweh ("He is" or "He causes to be") is the name God uses whenever He draws near us, reveals Himself personally, or enters into covenant. Through this personal relationship, we find victory! Through this personal relationship, we lose fear and gain confidence.

That story has stuck with me because it echoes the Father's heart. Living in victory isn't just about surviving trials or resisting sin; it's about intimacy with God. It's about looking into His eyes, face-to-face, heart to heart. Victory is not simply overcoming circumstances—it is walking in communion with the One who has already overcome.

Living in victory does not mean you never stumble. It means when you fall, you rise again, anchored in grace. It doesn't mean you never weep. It means your tears water seeds of hope. It doesn't mean battles vanish. It means you never fight alone.

I'll say it plainly: Victory is not something you achieve; it is something you receive. It is a gift, purchased by Christ on the cross and sealed by His resurrection. You don't earn it by effort; you embrace it by faith.

> *Victory is not something you achieve; it is*
> *something you receive.*

And when you do, your life becomes a testimony. People will see storms batter you and wonder why you stand. They will see trials that test you and marvel at your peace. And in that moment, your victory will point them to the Victor—Jesus Christ, the anchor who never fails.

FINAL WORD

More than four decades ago, a simple invitation anchored me to Christ. I didn't know then how much that decision would shape my journey—through joy and sorrow, loss and victory, questions and answers.

Being spiritually anchored doesn't mean you live without storms. It doesn't mean you won't face loss, grief, or disappointment. It means that when the storms come—and they will—your soul is secured to something deeper than circumstance, stronger than fear, greater than death.

Maybe you've been reading these words as a skeptic, unsure if any of this is for you. Let me say this: God's invitation is not limited to the religious or to the polished. He calls the weary, the broken, the uncertain, the sick, the thirsty. He calls people like the Samaritan woman at the well. He calls people like me, a young man searching for meaning in 1977. And He calls people like you.

The question is not whether storms will come; the question is what anchor will hold you when they do. Wealth will rust. Success will fade. Relationships, as precious as they are, cannot carry eternal weight. But Christ can. He is the same yesterday, today, and forever. His Word endures. His love never fails.

So here is my invitation to you: Don't drift away. Don't settle for shallow anchors. Drive your soul deep into the bedrock of Jesus Christ. Open His Word. Receive His forgiveness. Join His people. Live your faith. And stand in victory.

Now, in my fourth quarter of life, I am still learning, still growing, still being transformed. I haven't arrived, but I am anchored. And I can tell you with certainty: there is no greater security, no deeper peace, no truer hope.

The invitation is yours. The anchor is waiting. And the One who holds you will never let you go.

CHAPTER 7

A LESSON IN TEACHABILITY

By Dr. Charity Byers

I am a grateful visitor to Blessing Ranch, where Dr. Charity Byers and Dr. John Walker practice. It was when my brother, wife, and mother all died within eighteen months of one another that I was devastated, lost, and in great need of help! After my forty-hour intensive at the ranch—and with an additional ten to twenty hours of counseling when I came home—I became emotionally healthy again and ready, over time, to learn my new rhythm of life.

As the associate pastor at our church, it also took time to recapture my leadership gifts, which is why I want to share this chapter on a lesson in teachability, authored by Dr. Byers. She recently posted this article on the Blessing Ranch website as a blog.[1] I found this full of wisdom, guidance, and renewal, so I asked her to share it with our readers. So, whether you are in the fourth quarter and still working, retired, reenvisioning life, mentoring someone, or in need of a Christian perspective on

---

[1] Blessing Ranch Ministries, https://blessingranch.org

leadership, I feel strongly that you will benefit from its content on teachability.

Without teachability, our academic and personal growth is stunted, which promotes remaining in the past rather than living a full fourth quarter of life.

———

C ontinual learning is at the heart of lifelong discipleship— the kind of life Scripture calls us to as followers and leaders in Christ. Proverbs 9:9 reminds us to "Instruct the wise and they will be wiser still; teach the righteous and they will add to their learning." And in Proverbs 12:1, we're offered a clear truth: "Whoever loves discipline loves knowledge, but whoever hates correction is stupid." It couldn't be said any plainer than that.

THE POSTURE OF A TEACHABLE LEADER

Teachability relates to the humble, hungry spirit of a learner— someone who acknowledges the limits of their own wisdom and honors God's design for ongoing transformation. It's not just a helpful trait in leadership, it's a safeguard. A teachable heart keeps us surrendered to the voice of the Holy Spirit.

A teachable leader is:

- **Strong**, yet strength is submitted.
- **Wise**, yet wisdom is multiplied by many godly voices.
- **Experienced**, yet their experience is not assumed to be a perfect predictor of the future.
- **Influential**, yet also deeply influenced.

WHY LEADERS LOSE TEACHABILITY

There are many reasons leaders can become unteachable:

- **They're tired or comfortable**, and the effort of learning feels too heavy.
- **Pride has snuck in,** convincing them they are here to give but not to receive.
- **Insecurity is leading,** making them fear that admitting weakness might shatter the image of competence they've built.
- **They have defined leadership incorrectly** as a role built only on competency.

As a growing leader, you likely won't get noticed if you don't take charge, show what you know, and influence others. However, what it takes to appear like a leader is not always what it takes to become one.

> *What it takes to appear like a leader is not always what it takes to become one.*

A LESSON IN TEACHABILITY

Dr. Charity shared this story with me about her father, Dr. John Walker, founder of Blessing Ranch Ministries, who shared it with her from his training as a psychologist:

> Toward the end of my PhD program, I faced an oral defense—an intense examination of my knowledge and competency. Just before it began, my professor pulled me aside and said, 'John, I'm not going to let you out

of that room until I hear you say, "I don't know" three times.' His words didn't make sense to me. I went in ready to prove how much I knew.

About an hour into the exam, I found myself cornered by a question I couldn't answer. Discouraged, I admitted, 'I don't know.' The professor replied, 'Okay, let's move on.' A half hour later, it happened again, turning discouragement to despair: 'I don't know.' And again: 'Okay, let's move on.'

Then it clicked. I remembered what my professor had said as we were walking into the room. When the next question came, I confidently said, 'I don't know.' This time, they all smiled and said, 'Congratulations—you passed with flying colors.'

They taught me something invaluable: Teachability matters more than competency. You can't know everything—and it never helps to fake it. I needed humility that day—and a spirit of teachability for a lifetime.

THE FREEDOM IN "I DON'T KNOW"

There's no freer feeling than saying "I don't know." It releases us from the pressure of perfection, from the grip of pride, and from the fear of letting others see our limits. It is not weakness—it's surrender. It acknowledges the infinite wisdom of our Creator, which we cannot replicate or contain.

Jesus, though filled with wisdom, modeled a teachable spirit through his continual prayer, deep listening, and obedient submission to the Father. If Christ demonstrated a hunger to receive, how much more should we?

A TEACHABLE SPIRIT CHECK-IN

Ask yourself:

- Do I ask questions as often as I give answers?
- Do I seek input before making decisions?
- Do I act on meaningful feedback?
- Has anyone told me I'm stubborn or hard to correct?
- Do I feel like a failure when I admit I don't know something?

If your answers reveal a need for greater teachability, remember that growth begins with awareness.

HOW TO STAY TEACHABLE

- **Practice curiosity.** Ask questions even when you think you understand or know the answer.
- **Get into counseling or coaching,** not necessarily because you're in crisis, but to gain perspective.
- **Read your Bible as if it's speaking to you.** Don't let yourself read only for preparation. Read to hear the personal and direct voice of God guiding you.
- **Intentionally listen before you speak.** Challenge yourself to let at least two others speak before you in group settings.
- **Don't wait for feedback, ask for it.** Once a quarter, invite trusted voices to share what they believe God is trying to teach you.
- **Expose yourself to new things.** Learn something new. Read outside your specialty. Listen to a voice outside your normal circle of influence.

- **Deeply consider what you hear.** Don't refute immediately, reflect deeply. Consider what you hear as if it might be valuable before you respond to it.

A PRAYER FOR TEACHABILITY

Lord, help me never forget my need for your wisdom. Free me from pride, insecurity, and anything that hinders the teachable spirit you require of me. May my leadership be grounded in learning and listening—to you, and to those you've placed around me. Make me humble. Make me hungry. Shape me in your image. Amen.

May we, our families, workplaces, and communities be filled with leaders who are not ashamed to say, "I don't know—show me."

CHAPTER 8

LEAVING A LEGACY LETTER

By Pastor Rick Craig

Creating a legacy is the result of a lifetime of decision-making, shaping the story you leave behind—a written, oral, and lived history. Writing a legacy letter may take hours or even days of revisions, but its impact can resonate for generations.

Any legacy—good or bad—tells a story. Legacies develop over time, shaped by areas of life such as faith and spirituality, character and personal values, relationships and influence, acts of service, financial responsibility, wisdom from life's lessons, and education. Each of these aspects contributes to the personal and lasting impression we leave behind.

Clarity in life—whether in relationships, spiritual growth, vocational direction, or other areas—comes through reflection, examination, and adjustment. Writing a legacy letter follows the same process. Too often, we move through life reacting to circumstances rather than proactively shaping our journey (see chapter 4). We respond to challenges in the workplace, health concerns, financial burdens, and relationships without taking the time later to reflect deeply on our experiences.

This is why a legacy letter is so powerful. It provides an opportunity to express love and gratitude, and reflect on our life journey, core values and beliefs, and wisdom gained. We can also add prayers of blessing and unspoken thoughts—messages we want to leave for family, friends, colleagues, and communities.

Below are key areas to explore when crafting your legacy letter, making it a meaningful and intentional part of your lasting impact.

KEY AREAS TO INCLUDE IN YOUR LEGACY LETTER

1. Faith and Spirituality

As with all aspects of life, spiritual growth is a journey from immaturity to wisdom through experience, investment, and mentorship. This process, often referred to as spiritual formation, involves growing in faith and understanding our relationship with Christ and one another (Colossians 3:1–17).

In your legacy letter, share insights from your spiritual journey. What wisdom have you gained? What Scriptures guided you? How has faith shaped your decisions and relationships? For clarity: Faith provides the foundation—belief in God and the truths of Scripture—while spirituality is the active, personal expression of that faith. A deep faith leads to a transformed life, one marked by prayer, worship, and obedience to God.

2. Personal Values and Character Traits

The lessons learned through both successes and failures form a wellspring of wisdom. Personal values serve as guiding principles in life, while character traits shape how we approach challenges and relationships.

Use your legacy letter to pass on what you've learned. Share the significance of values such as accountability, balance, commitment, community, faithfulness, justice, love, and unity. Describe the character traits that shaped your decisions, such as compassion, patience, integrity, humility, resilience, perseverance, and service to others. Your reflections will help the next generation understand the motivations behind your actions and encourage them to cultivate these qualities in their own lives.

3. Relationships and Influence

The phrase "I love you" can carry different meanings. Sometimes, it's a routine farewell as we head out the door; other times, it's a deep and heartfelt declaration of affection. In your legacy letter, when you say, "I love you," take the time to explain why. This could provide much-needed clarity or affirm the depth of your feelings.

Make your letter personal by recognizing individuals by name rather than offering a broad statement. A heartfelt acknowledgment can have a profound effect on the recipient, making them feel valued and seen.

Reflect on how you have influenced others and how others have influenced you. Share these experiences in detail, as they can serve as motivational and affirming moments for those reading your letter.

4. Wisdom and Life Lessons

Life is filled with challenges, many of which are unavoidable. In your legacy letter, offer guidance and encouragement based on the lessons you've learned. Share insights on navigating relationships, career paths, faith struggles, or personal growth. Encourage recipients to continue learning, growing, and making a positive impact in their families and communities.

5. Acts of Service

Raising children often involves teachable moments, such as learning to say please and thank you. Beyond these basics, we also guide them to see the needs of others and take action. This, too, is part of a person's spiritual and personal growth.

Share in your legacy letter how serving others brought joy and purpose to your life. Reflect on why you chose certain acts of service and the impact they had on both you and those you served. If you know the recipient's passions or skills, encourage them to consider careers or volunteer work that aligns with their gifts. Making your message personal inspires action and nurtures purpose in those who read it.

6. Financial Responsibility

Your legacy letter is not meant to be a victory lap celebrating wise investments but rather a heartfelt reflection on financial wisdom, stewardship, and generosity. Share how your financial decisions reflected your values and priorities. Offer advice on financial planning, generosity, and the importance of wills or trusts.

7. Education and Its Application

Education—whether academic, vocational, or self-directed learning—is a valuable tool for personal and professional growth. Use your legacy letter to encourage younger generations to explore their talents, seek vocational alignment, and embrace lifelong learning. (See chapter 4 for additional insight on vocational alignment.)

Mentoring young people in this area is an act of service that will be deeply appreciated in the years to come. Offer guidance that helps them avoid mistakes and make informed decisions about their future.

8. Legacy of Forgiveness and Reconciliation

Unresolved conflicts can burden both the living and the departed. A legacy letter provides an opportunity to offer or seek forgiveness, promoting peace and healing among loved ones. If there are relationships in need of reconciliation, use your letter as a means to express your desire for restoration and unity.

9. Hopes and Blessings for Future Generations

Take a moment to write blessings for your children, grandchildren, and future descendants. Express your hopes for their lives, their character, and their faith. A simple message like, "My hope for you is that you will always pursue truth, love others well, and live with integrity," can be a guiding light for those who come after you.

LEGACY LETTER: WRITTEN OR VIDEO FORMAT?

With today's technology, you have options for how to preserve your legacy letter:

- A written format allows for personal, detailed notes to individuals.
- A video format can incorporate stories, reflections, and prayers, bringing your words to life in a deeply personal way.

Having both formats ensures your message is preserved in a heartfelt, engaging, and accessible manner for your loved ones.

Guidance on Distribution and Storage

Consider how and when you want your legacy letter to be shared. Should it be read privately or at a memorial service? Where should it be stored? Entrust it to someone reliable to ensure your message reaches its intended recipients.

Why a Legacy Letter Matters

As I write this book, I have officiated well over 265 funerals and memorials. The most profound impact I have witnessed comes from individuals who made an intentional effort to communicate with their loved ones before passing.

Whether through verbal conversations, a written legacy letter, a recorded video, hidden notes for loved ones to find, or a final letter to be read at a service, expressing your thoughts before it's too late leaves a lasting impression. I strongly encourage you to take the next step in completing your legacy. Be creative, be intentional, and make your message known.

A Sample Legacy Letter

To assist you in writing your legacy letter, I have authored a letter that my father "may have written" to our family. Because of my personal interaction with him, and watching him with my brother and mum, I can say with confidence that its contents are heart filled, accurate, and lingering, just as a legacy letter could be.

I listed headings for each section to assist you in writing your letter. You may choose to leave the headings in or remove them; it's a personal choice.

My Dearest Irene, Rob, and Rick,

If you're reading this, then my time on this earth has come to an end. I want you to know that my love for you is eternal, and my heart is filled with gratitude for the life we shared. I may be gone, but my spirit will always be with you—in the laughter we shared, in the lessons I taught you, and in the love that binds us together.

Faith and Spirituality

Faith has been my quiet foundation, the steady force that carried me through the hardships of World War II while defending our country, the struggles of work, and the joys of family. Though I was never a preacher like your grandfather, nor a scholar, I believed in God's presence in my life. I saw him in the kindness of strangers, in the beauty of nature, and in the strength of my wife and sons. When life was uncertain, I turned to prayer, sometimes in words, other times in silent hope. I leave you with this: Trust in God's plan, even when it doesn't make sense. Love him, love others, and walk with integrity because we hold God's reputation in the palm of our hands.

Personal Values and Character Traits

I wasn't an educated man, but I knew the value of honesty, hard work, and kindness. Life wasn't always easy, but I learned that patience and perseverance made the difference between despair and hope. To my sons, I hope you carry these values forward. Be men of your word. Treat others with respect. When life knocks you down, get up and try again.

Relationships and Influence

Rob and Rick, you were my pride and joy. Watching you grow into men has been my greatest accomplishment. I may not have been a perfect father, but I hope I showed you how to be kind, strong, and responsible. My love for you is without condition. I hope you remember our moments together—the times I taught you how to fix things, the nights we spent laughing at the dinner table, and the times I held you close when you were afraid.

Never doubt how much I love you. And never be afraid to say those words to the people who matter most to you. Love should never be left unspoken. Share it because it's one of life's greatest gifts!

And Irene, my love, you have been the best part of my life. Your gentleness and unwavering support made every struggle worth it. You are the greatest gift God ever gave me, and I pray you always know how deeply I cherish you.

Wisdom and Life Lessons

Life will test you, boys. It will challenge you in ways you never expect. My advice? Face each trial with courage. Work hard, be honest, and never take shortcuts. There is dignity in labor, whether you're fixing a broken pipe or chasing a dream. And remember, failure isn't the end—it's a lesson. Learn from it, get back up, and keep moving forward.

Acts of Service

One of life's greatest joys is helping others. If a neighbor needs a hand, give it. If a stranger is struggling, offer kindness. If someone is hungry, feed them. I found purpose in fixing things—not just broken machines, but also broken spirits. A simple act of kindness can change a life. Don't be too busy to care.

Financial Responsibility

Money isn't everything, but how you manage it matters. I worked hard to provide for our family, and I hope you do the same for yours. Remember the lesson I taught you about money: Give your first 10 percent to God, then save the next 10 percent, and finally, live off the remainder. True wealth is found in the love of family and friends, not in a bank account, but prudence is wisdom.

Education and Lifelong Learning

Though I never had the chance for formal schooling, I learned through experience, observation, and hard work. Never stop learning. Read, ask questions, and be curious about the world. Education isn't just found in books but also in the lessons life teaches you every day. Pay attention.

Legacy of Forgiveness and Reconciliation

If I have ever wronged you, I ask for your forgiveness. Life is too short to carry grudges. If there are wounds that need healing, may this letter be the beginning of that process. Love each other, forgive each other, and don't let pride keep you apart.

Hopes and Blessings for Future Generations

Rob and Rick, I pray that you live lives filled with purpose and joy. Be good husbands, good fathers, and good men. Love deeply, work hard, and never take a single day for granted.

To Irene, my love, thank you for walking this life with me. You were my heart, my home, my safe place. I will love you always.

I leave you with this: Live with love, lead with kindness, and never stop believing in the goodness of people. My legacy isn't in the work I did, but in the love I gave. Carry it forward.

With all my love,

Bob Craig

ABOUT THE AUTHOR

Richard J. Craig
Ordained Christian pastor,
author, and certified life coach

Vocational Background

Before being called into full-time ministry, I spent twenty-five years in the business world—first as an employee, then as the owner of two separate businesses. My vocational calling into pastoral ministry came later in life than most—at age forty-four—which led me back to school for two and a half years to prepare for this new season of life.

Prior to retiring in 2019, I had the privilege of serving as an associate pastor and later as a campus pastor for eighteen years. I oversaw both church and school operations on a shared campus, led eleven ministries, and supported our community through counseling, officiating funeral and memorial services, and, on occasion, serving with the local chaplaincy. Those years not only shaped my leadership style but also deepened my heart for caring for people in every season of life.

Professional Experience

- Twenty-six years of full-time pastoral ministry, serving in Laguna Niguel, Napa, and the greater Bay Area of Northern California
- Leadership of eleven ministries, including oversight of church and Christian school operations
- Certified life coach, specializing in legacy development and end-of-life care
- Officiant for over 265 memorial and funeral services—including those honoring military veterans, law enforcement officers, firefighters, and civilians at Sacramento Valley National Cemetery and throughout the Bay Area of Northern California.
- Author of the *When It's Time®* series:

  — *When It's Time®: End-of-Life Planning at Any Age—Make It Part of Your Legacy*
  — *When It's Time®: An End-of-Life Workbook for Pre-Planners and Survivors*
  — *When It's Time®: Leader's Guide—Leading Your Group Through End-of-Life Pre-Planning and Survivor Support*
  — *6 Hallmarks of a Fantastic Fourth Quarter: Your Master Plan for Finishing Strong*

Educational Background

- Bachelor of Arts, Vanguard University
- Certified life coach, Western Seminary
- Certified facilitator, Prepare / Enrich Ministry
- Ordained Christian pastor

Current Residence

Fairfield, California

What I Enjoy About My Work

Serving others has always been the heartbeat of my calling. There is no greater joy than walking alongside people in moments of celebration and sorrow—especially helping families navigate loss with compassion, dignity, and hope. Officiating funerals and memorials remains one of the most sacred expressions of my ministry. I count it an honor to help others find peace, purpose, and spiritual grounding in life's most vulnerable moments.

Even in retirement, I remain energized by writing, speaking, facilitating seminars, training at hospitals and hospice organizations, being a guest on webinars and podcasts, and coaching others toward finishing life well—with intentionality, grace, and unwavering faith.

A Piece of Wisdom: Living Well in the Fourth Quarter

The concluding chapter of life isn't about slowing down but about narrowing your focus on what truly matters. Embrace your faith, cherish your family, and live each day as if it were a letter being written to those who come after you. There is still time to inspire, to forgive, to bless, and to finish strong.

Contact Info

- Website: https://whenitstime.org
- Email: pastorrickcraig@whenitstime.org

CONTRIBUTING AUTHORS

A TRIBUTE TO WISDOM SHARED

One of the greatest blessings in life is to walk alongside others who are deeply committed to living well, finishing strong, and serving with purpose. Within the pages of this book, I have shared timeless principles that guide us into a meaningful and impactful fourth quarter of life. But I am not alone on this journey. I have had the honor of collaborating with six exceptional individuals: Charity, John, Bill, Lynne, Scott, and Kent—men and women who embody the very hallmarks this book celebrates.

These contributing authors are not only respected professionals in their individual fields, but they're also seasoned by life, driven by conviction, and rich in wisdom. Their credentials are impressive, with years of formal education, professional expertise, and a consistent record of service to others. Yet what truly sets them apart is not just their knowledge, but also their character. They are generous with their time, intentional in their relationships, and grounded in purpose.

Each contributor brings a unique perspective to this collective work, and their insights add tremendous depth to the message of finishing well. They have not simply written from theory, but from a wealth of experience—what I would call "legacy-rich living." Their lives are a testimony to leadership, resilience, stewardship, and faithful service. These are people who have not only made a living but have made a life.

In the pages that follow, you will find a short biography of each author. Four of the six have quick-response (QR) codes linking to their professional websites or resources, allowing you to connect more personally with their stories, services, and wisdom. I strongly encourage you to take advantage of these links. Whether you're looking for guidance, mentorship, or inspiration, these individuals have much to offer.

To each of these friends and fellow sojourners—thank you. Your voice in this book is a gift, your life is a model, and your legacy is a blessing to all who have the privilege of knowing you.

AUTHORS

John M. Walker, PhD is an ordained Christian Pastor, retired psychologist, and author.

Charity M. Byers, PhD is a psychologist and author.

Vocational Background

Before becoming a licensed psychologist, Dr. Walker spent ten years in ministry serving as a local pastor. After receiving his PhD in counseling psychology in 1985, Dr. Walker worked as a psychologist in private practice in Houston, Texas. As the founder of Blessing Ranch Ministries, Dr. Walker spent his later career investing in the hearts and lives of Christian leaders through intensive counseling.

As Dr. Walker's youngest daughter, Dr. Byers grew up watching her parents build and serve Blessing Ranch Ministries. Upon completion of her doctoral education, it was her privilege to join her father as a fellow licensed psychologist at Blessing Ranch Ministries, helping Christian leaders live well, lead well, and finish well.

Professional Experience

- Dr. Walker and Dr. Byers coauthored the books *Unhindered: Aligning the Story of your Heart* and *Unhindered 30 Days: Discover Healing, Freedom, and Power Within.*
- Dr. Walker and Dr. Byers (in partnership with Dr. Greg Wiens of Healthy Growing Leaders) developed the Unhindered Clinical Instrument, an assessment tool that measures emotional and spiritual health.

- Since 1996, Blessing Ranch Ministries has helped guide over 4,000 leaders into greater health.

Educational Background

Dr. Walker

- Bachelor of Arts, Christian ministry, Lincoln Christian University
- Master of Arts, psychology and religion, Butler University and Christian Theological Seminary
- PhD, counseling psychology, Indiana State University
- Ordained Christian pastor

Dr. Byers

- Bachelor of Arts, clinical, counseling, and school psychology, Western State College of Colorado
- Master of Arts, general psychology, University of Northern Colorado
- PhD, counseling psychology, University of Denver

Current Residence

Trinity, Florida

What We Enjoy About Our Work

It is a privilege to see others come to know what it's like to live more freely and lightly. By finding new life-giving perspectives and being freed from hindrances, we get to witness despair turn into hope, self-sabotage give way to self-leadership, and helplessness become empowerment. We get to watch others become better versions of themselves, and in turn, become a greater blessing to others. It inspires us not to become complacent but to continually pursue growth and health.

A Piece of Wisdom: Living Well in the Fourth Quarter

Even if others don't honor you for the sacrifices you've made, know that they've been worth it.

Even if the world doesn't seek your well-earned wisdom, be thankful for who it's made you.

Even if you carry many scars, notice the strength they've left in you.

Even if you're tired, know you still have a difference to make.

Even if life disappoints you, appreciate what can't be taken from you.

Contact Info

Website: www.blessingranch.org
Email: info@blessingranch.org

Author Dr. William "Bill" Nesbitt III

Vocational Background

Dr. William R. Nesbitt III has over four decades of distinguished medical practice, with his expertise in end-of-life care grounded in compassionate service to thousands of patients and families during their most vulnerable moments. This extensive experience provides the foundation for his authoritative writing on aging, health management, and the medical realities of life's final chapter.

Professional Experience

- Dr. Nesbitt's diverse medical career spans emergency medicine, family practice with obstetrics, and specialized end-of-life care. He spent five years as a full-time emergency physician with Sacramento Emergency Medical Group, serving as their base station medical director for multiple ambulance services. His entrepreneurial spirit led him to found Nesbitt Enterprises in the 1980s, a medical equipment R&D company, where he earned five US patents for innovative medical devices.
- As a nationally recognized leader in hospice medicine, Dr. Nesbitt has served as the hospice medical director for major healthcare systems, including Sutter Health, Vitas Hospice, and Providence Healthcare. Most recently, he founded Providence Healthcare's Program of All-inclusive Care for the Elderly (PACE) in Napa, California, before transitioning to focus on research and writing.

Educational Background

- A 1977 graduate of UC Davis School of Medicine, Dr. Nesbitt completed his family practice residency at San Joaquin County Hospital, where he served as house staff president. Board certified in family medicine since 1980, he has earned additional certifications in geriatric medicine, long-term care, and hospice and palliative medicine and served as a certified hospice medical director.

Current Residence

Green Valley, California

What I Enjoy About My Work

Dr. Nesbitt's adventurous spirit extends beyond his professional life. A PADI-certified SCUBA diver and automotive enthusiast, he has built award-winning custom cars and restored classic automobiles. In the 1990s, he combined his love of fishing with his communication skills as a monthly columnist for *West Coast Fisherman Forecast News*, writing "Fishin' for Fun with Doc Nesbitt."

Currently retired from active medical practice, Dr. Nesbitt lives in Northern California with his wife, a retired elementary school teacher. They have two grown children who work in Napa, and three grandchildren. This personal experience with family relationships across generations enriches his understanding of the challenges and opportunities that define life's fourth quarter.

A Piece of Wisdom: Living Well in the Fourth Quarter

Dr. Nesbitt believes that aging well requires intentional preparation—physical, emotional, and spiritual. His chapter "Physically Fit" reflects his conviction that the fourth quarter of life can go beyond just surviving and truly be enjoyed when approached with wisdom, planning, and the right mindset. His medical expertise, combined with his pastoral heart and practical wisdom, makes him an ideal guide for readers seeking to finish strong and live their remaining years with purpose, health, and dignity.

Contact Info

Email: wnesbittmd@hotmail.com.

Author Lynne Nachtrieb

Registered dietitian and certified specialist in
oncology nutrition

Professional Experience

- Oncology dietitian, Leonard Cancer Institute at Mission Hospital, Mission Viejo, California
- Clinical dietitian, Mission Hospital, Mission Viejo, California
- Dietitian, private practice, Counseling Associates, Mission Viejo, California
- Weight management nutrition counselor, Rosecrans Obesity Care Medical Clinic, Norwalk, California

Educational Background

BA, foods and nutrition, California State University, San Diego, California

Current Residence

Fort Collins, Colorado

What I Enjoy About My Work

Educating and supporting others to achieve their health goals through nutrition, whether during times of illness or wellness. What we eat is critical to our health and well-being. I enjoy helping people understand science-based nutrition information to navigate the massive misinformation found on the internet, social media, and books, or via untrained "specialists."

A Piece of Wisdom: Living Well in the Fourth Quarter

During cancer treatment, optimizing nutrition can prevent loss of muscle tissue, maintain weight, and minimize nutritional impact symptoms such as nausea, vomiting, lack of appetite, and taste changes. The patient is better able to tolerate treatment, has an improved quality of life, and learns specific strategies to get back to health once treatment is complete. Supporting patients with their nutritional needs also enables them to have some control in a positive way during a very difficult time of life. This requires a personalized approach because each of us is a unique individual with unique needs and desires.

Author Scott Couchenour

Certified executive coach, business coach

Vocational Background

Scott Couchenour brings over twenty years of executive leadership and entrepreneurial experience to his role as a fourth-quarter strategy coach. Having served as both COO and CEO, he has firsthand knowledge of the demands, decisions, and dynamics that shape a business leader's career. Through his own professional transition and the founding of Serving Strong Enterprises, Scott has channeled his operational expertise into a calling—helping fellow leaders move from business success to personal significance. His vocational history informs his coaching with credibility, insight, and a deep understanding of what it takes to lead well through life's pivotal seasons.

Professional Experience

- Over two decades of experience in executive leadership roles (COO and CEO)
- Founder of Serving Strong Enterprises, LLC
- Executive coach specializing in fourth-quarter leaders (ages 45+)
- Strategist for business owners and executives navigating career transitions
- Developer of a proprietary framework built on six hallmarks for life design
- Advisor to transition teams addressing the personal side of business exits
- Partner to financial advisors, wealth planners, and exit-planning professionals

- Facilitator of 1:1 intensives, coaching groups, and strategy sessions
- Speaker on topics related to purpose, legacy, and post-career fulfillment
- Guide for leaders creating personalized strategic life plans rooted in clarity and legacy

Educational Background

- BA, Sociology, Mount Vernon Nazarene University / Youngstown State University
- Certified life coach, Institute for Life Coach Training

Current Residence

Salem, Ohio

What I Enjoy About My Work

I feel a deep sense of calling to be a steward of my story—in particular, the loss of my career, income, and identity upon closing our second-generation family-owned business at age fifty. This experience, combined with the coaching experience and tenure as COO and CEO, allows me to help leaders build a way of living that is by design, not by default.

The greatest sense of fulfillment is derived from knowing that the work I get to do with my clients is helping increase the impact that they will have on the world for good. Adding to that, knowing that they are more fulfilled in life and are reducing regret is an added benefit.

A Piece of Wisdom: Living Well in the Fourth Quarter

Make it your main ambition to eliminate as much living by default as you can. Living by default results in higher regret.

Contact Info

Website: https://www.servingstrong.com
Email: coach@servingstrong.com

AUTHOR KENT KUHLMANN

Wealth manager, financial counselor,
and certified exit planning advisor

Professional Experience

With thirty-five years as a financial advisor, I guide clients through the complex financial challenges, emotional money blocks, and victories that define their lives. My career began in real estate investments, evolved into life and health insurance, and expanded into portfolio management. This diverse background equips me to support clients through significant life transitions—both joyful and challenging—with expertise and empathy.

As a certified exit-planning advisor (CEPA), I specialize in helping business owners maximize their enterprise's value and navigate successful transitions while securing their financial future. Having personally experienced many of these transitions, I bring a unique perspective and deep compassion to my work. As an independent advisor, I prioritize my clients' needs, exploring tailored solutions free from institutional constraints.

Education and Credentials

- BA, San Diego State University
- Accredited investment fiduciary (AIF)
- Certified exit-planning advisor (CEPA)

These qualifications, combined with decades of hands-on experience, enable me to provide strategic, fiduciary-driven guidance to my clients.

What I Love About My Work

The financial markets are unpredictable, but life's challenges and triumphs are deeply personal. I find immense reward in coaching clients through major transitions—whether helping a widow navigate loss or guiding a business owner through a successful exit. As a "financial sherpa," I draw on my experience to lighten a client's load and guide them along the safest path to their goals. Having walked these paths myself, I'm committed to making a meaningful difference in their financial journey.

A Piece of Wisdom: Living Well in the Fourth Quarter

True joy often lies in life's simplest moments. In your later years, resist society's pressure to stay overly structured. Reflect on what truly makes you happy, revisit the passions that feed your soul, and embrace the time you've earned. Time is your most precious asset—use it wisely.

Location

Napa Valley, CA

Contact

Website: www.avior.com/locations/wealth-management-
napa-ca
Email: kent.kuhlmann@avior.com

OTHER BOOKS
BY RICK CRAIG

Death is a journey everyone will experience, yet it is seldom discussed. Instead, survivors are left to navigate it on their own, unequipped and paralyzed by the loss of a loved one.

When It's Time walks through thirteen end-of-life realities that surviving family members will inevitably encounter. This book offers detailed information for "pre-need" situations, when you are planning before death, and "at-need" situations, when death has occurred.

With personal stories of loss, along with insight from contributing authors who are experts in their fields, *When It's Time* is a relatable guide to equip anyone to take the next steps in end-of-life planning. Discover how a well-planned strategy can be one of the most valuable gifts for your loved ones, becoming an integral part of your legacy.

The *When It's Time* **workbook** contains relatable stories, as well as insight from contributing authors who are experts in their field, to equip anyone to take the next steps in end-of-life planning. This companion workbook serves as a guide, offering practical action steps, templates, and checklists to help you develop or implement an end-of-life plan, including: gathering your personal information, assembling a support team, calculating your life insurance needs, choosing a trustee and powers of attorney, registering and applying for benefits, deciding on disposition, writing your obituary, planning a funeral or memorial service, and more.

The leader's guide will equip you to become an effective group facilitator by empowering you to lead discussions, share pertinent information, and answer questions. With a step-by-step blueprint for your group gathering, highlighted points of interest, and discussion questions coordinated with the book content, you'll have all the tools you need to guide your group members to make wise decisions.